Techniques for Teachers

Techniques for Teachers

A Guide for Nonnative Speakers of English

Ann Wennerstrom

Ann Arbor

THE UNIVERSITY OF MICHIGAN PRESS

Copyright © 1989 by Ann Wennerstrom
Editorial compilation and new material copyright © by the University of Michigan 1991
All rights reserved
ISBN 0-472-08148-9
Library of Congress Catalog Card No. 90-72021
Published in the United States of America by
The University of Michigan Press
Manufactured in the United States of America

1994   1993   1992   1991   4   3   2   1

Graphic work by April Ryan

No part of this book may be reproduced or transmitted in any form or by any means, electronic or mechanical, including photocopying, recording, or by any information storage or retrieval system without written permission of the publisher.

All transcripts from the videotape *Techniques for Teachers: A Guide for Nonnative Speakers of English,* copyright © 1989 by Ann Wennerstrom, are printed with permission.

For Andy

Acknowledgments

I am pleased to acknowledge Joan Morley, Rita Wong, and Judy Gilbert, whose work has been an inspiration to me over the years.

I would like to thank Daphne Mackey and Bill Harshbarger for their continued support and advice throughout the development of this project. I would also like to thank Carla Stern for her careful work on the manuscript.

I am grateful to April Ryan, Sandra Wells, John Givens, Bill Hevly, Jack Armstrong, and all the rest of the folks at the University of Washington Instructional Media Services for their expertise and enthusiasm for this project.

For many other helpful ideas and suggestions, I am especially grateful to Sandra Silberstein, Kathryn Hall Allahyari, Barbara Bell, Pat Grogan, Barbara Hansen-Johnston, Anita Sökmen, Karen Freisam, and Debra Siquiera. I would also like to thank Cheríe Lenz-Hackett for her help with the computer.

A huge round of applause goes to June Morita, Cara Izumi, Sharon Büllen, and all the rest of the cast of the videotape: Douglas Brown, Patty Heiser, Sharon Kita, Tim Teigen, Wade Pickett, Jim Ward, Becky Boon Mills, Kate Hammond, Bob Messina, Rob Fieser, Cynthia Howe, Andrew Starcher, Elisabeth Mitchell, Lesley Lin, Laura Kelsey, and Leslie Jabusch. You are the greatest!

I would also like to extend a special thanks to all of my students in the ITA training course for letting me know their needs and for field testing these materials.

Finally, thanks ever and ever so much to my family, Bonnie, Clara, and Andy, and to Colleen Walker for child-care.

Contents

Introduction   xi

Part I. Lectures

1. Introductions 3
2. Transitions 13
3. Restating and Summarizing...........25
4. Definitions 33
5. Examples............................43
6. Graphs and Diagrams 53

Part II. Classroom Interaction

7. Student Questions 1 75
8. Student Questions 2 83
9. Brainstorming 91
10. Problem Solving 99
11. Discussion.........................107
12. Putting Students to Work 119

Part III. Office Hours

13. One on One: Interacting with Individuals....................129

Part IV. Pronunciation

    14.   Consonants 151
    15.   Vowels 163

Appendixes

    1.   Discussions on American Culture 185
    2.   "Teachers in Action" Transcripts 189

Index 213

Introduction

Techniques for Teachers is a complete English language course with a workbook and video program. It was developed as a core text for an International Teaching Assistant (ITA) training course at the University of Washington, where it continues to be used successfully. *Techniques for Teachers* is also useful as a self-study guide for foreign teaching professionals in the United States and Canada. Professors and college teachers, as well as ITAs who wish to improve their English skills, will find the *Techniques for Teachers* program invaluable. It is interesting, practical, and user-friendly.

The main goal of *Techniques for Teachers* is to improve the English fluency of nonnative speakers, especially teachers. By watching the video, viewers see U.S. teachers in a university classroom, actively engaged in the teaching process. They hear the language associated with different aspects of teaching, and, by doing the activities in the workbook, they learn to analyze the language of the teachers and to practice and improve their own English skills. The result is more fluent English in the classroom, a better understanding of classroom dynamics, and greater self-confidence.

The Video

The *Techniques for Teachers* video is organized into three main parts: Lecturing, Classroom Interaction, and Office Hours. In parts I and II, each unit highlights a different aspect of classroom teaching, such as giving a definition, answering student questions, or leading a discussion. On the screen, viewers see short excerpts of classes in Statistics, Mathematics, and Business. With the help of a narrator, they learn how the English language functions in these lessons. In part III, Office Hours, viewers see five different scenes of teachers in conference with students in their office. In each scene, the students have special problems that the teachers try to resolve. The emphasis here is on one-to-one communication skills.

The Workbook

The *Techniques for Teachers* workbook expands and enhances the video. Each unit brings out the main features of the English language as it is used by the teachers in the videotape. The workbook also provides explanations, exercises, and other activities to improve English fluency while increasing understanding of classroom procedures. In addition, the workbook includes two units that focus specifically on the pronunciation of English sounds. Two appendixes contain discussion questions on American culture and complete transcriptions of the lessons on the videotape.

Suggestions for ITA Trainers

Techniques for Teachers was developed for ITA training. Each unit covers a different aspect of teaching with useful activities for practice. What follows is a synopsis of the main activities in the workbook and suggestions for their use.

Teachers in Action

A typical unit of *Techniques for Teachers* workbook begins with a section called Teachers in Action. In this section, a particular aspect of teaching is introduced, such as giving a definition or leading a discussion. By watching the video, ITAs see examples of U.S. teachers engaged in that aspect of teaching. The workbook provides guidelines and focus questions that help ITAs understand what the teachers on the video are doing. Of course, it is easy to rewind the video and play it more than once for better understanding.

Language Models, key sentences used by the teachers on the video, are also singled out and printed in the workbook. By reviewing these model sentences, ITAs may find language they can use in their own teaching situations. For ITAs who want even more detail on the language, the complete transcripts of the video are printed in appendix 2.

Some trainers may choose to do the Teachers in Action activity in class. Others may assign it as homework. By putting the video on reserve at a library or media center, trainers can ask ITAs to watch it themselves, answering the questions in the workbook while they watch.

Speech Patterns

Most units also include one or more Speech Patterns sections, in which common patterns of English are explained. Most of the Speech Patterns sections present material on the intonation patterns of English, including word stress, contrastive stress, and pauses. In some units, there is material on grammar or vocabulary as it pertains to a particular aspect of teaching. For example, in the unit 6, "Graphs and Diagrams," there is a Speech Patterns section on how to read mathematical formulas. In a unit on "Student Questions," the Speech Patterns section presents material on the sentence stress of questions.

Fluency Work

ITAs are taught to incorporate each unit's Speech Patterns into their own speech through a series of Fluency Work activities, which fall into three major categories. In the first, ITAs listen to the video and carefully analyze the written transcript of the speaker's words, following the guidelines in the workbook. Then they practice reading the words aloud to get a feel for the speech patterns of the native speaker. This is not simply an oral reading activity; it is meant to be a detailed analysis, rather like an actor practicing lines for the theater. It is a good idea to do this activity with audiotapes, encouraging ITAs to develop their own fluency.

In the second type of Fluency Work activity, an outline of information is given that ITAs are to announce out loud in their own words. Using their own phrasing, they concentrate on fluent English. This activity may be done with audiotapes, or it can be used to practice presentation skills in front of the class.

A final type of Fluency Work activity is Speech Analysis. Here, ITAs tape-record their own free speech and transcribe it, writing down their words. From this transcript, they can locate problems and make improvements. This empowers the ITA to take charge of his or her own English language development. ITAs who are currently teaching a class are encouraged to audiotape material from their own classes for the Speech Analysis.

Miniclass Assignment

Most units of the workbook also include a Miniclass Assignment in which the ITAs perform a five-to-ten-minute teaching activity. In these short activities, they can integrate all the skills they have worked on, while concentrating on the particular aspects of teaching presented in the unit. A Vocabulary Planner is provided in the workbook so that ITAs can identify those words that may be difficult for them to pronounce. By practicing them before their miniclass, they can incorporate pronunciation work into their teaching.

It is recommended that these miniclasses be videotaped or audiotaped so that ITAs can view them afterward, following the Self-Evaluation Form. This form contains questions that help ITAs analyze their own lessons. It may also be used by other class members to give feedback to their peers. ITA trainers who wish to give feedback on miniclasses may use this form as well, or they may follow the Trainer Feedback Guidelines in unit 1.

By the end of each unit of *Techniques for Teachers,* ITAs have had thorough exposure to and practice with a particular aspect of teaching. They have seen native speakers demonstrate teaching techniques on the video, analyzed the language of the native speakers, practiced using the language themselves, and, finally, performed a short teaching activity that integrates all the new skills they have learned.

Suggestions for Self-Study

If you are teaching at a North American university or college and English is not your native language, *Techniques for Teachers* may be just what you need to brush up on your English skills. It is easy to use *Techniques for Teachers.* You can play the videotape in your own home while you do the workbook activities to improve your English. If you do not have a videotape player, you can probably find one at your campus library or media center.

The videotape shows U.S. faculty engaged in the teaching process. By seeing and hearing these teachers and by reading the printed text of their words, you can learn more about the language of the classroom. Exercises in the workbook teach you how to analyze the language that you hear on the screen. Other workbook activities allow you to practice speaking. In fact, if you are teaching now, you can easily adapt the exercises in *Techniques for Teachers* to your own individual teaching situation. There is a strong emphasis on

English fluency for the classroom and on presentation skills. Following are some suggestions for how to use this workbook for self-study.

Start each unit by previewing the workbook, looking through the unit to see what will be covered. Then play the video for the unit, rewinding it as many times as you wish. Follow the guidelines and answer the questions in the Teachers in Action section. Also notice the Language Models section of the workbook. In this section, some of the most useful language from the video is singled out. Perhaps you can use some of these phrases in your own teaching. Remember that there are transcripts in appendix 2 to help you understand the video in even more detail.

Now read the Speech Patterns sections of the unit. These give careful explanations of pronunciation and intonation patterns, grammar or vocabulary, all pertaining to the English of the classroom. Next, you will find a series of Fluency Work exercises in which you have the opportunity to practice what you have learned in the unit. It is recommended that you purchase a small tape recorder; tape-record your own voice as you do the Fluency Work exercises and then play the recording back. Try it several times until you are satisfied with your own progress.

The Speech Analysis is particularly well suited to individual work. Here, you tape-record your own speech and transcribe it, writing down every word. From this transcript, you can locate problems and make improvements. Detailed instructions for how to do the Speech Analysis can be found in each unit of the workbook. Those who are currently teaching a class are encouraged to tape-record material from their own classes for the Speech Analysis.

Techniques for Teachers also contains a series of Miniclass Assignments. Each assignment highlights a different aspect of teaching. These assignments can easily be applied to a real classroom situation by following the directions for the assignment in your own class. Videotape or audiotape the class and play it back later, using the Self-Evaluation Form. This form contains questions to help you look objectively at what you did in class.

Overall, *Techniques for Teachers* works very well for self-study because the video does the talking. With the emphasis on individual work and self-analysis, you can start at your own level of English and progress from there. By seeing and hearing the U.S. teachers on the screen, by doing the exercises in the workbook, and by practicing your skills while you teach your own classes, you can make a great improvement in your English.

Supplementary Material

Techniques for Teachers also features some useful supplementary material. This includes two units on pronunciation, discussion questions, and transcripts of the video. A brief description of each of these follows.

Pronunciation

Part IV of *Techniques for Teachers* concentrates on pronunciation of the sounds of English. It begins with an overview of strategies for how to improve spoken English by integrating pronunciation work into other aspects of speaking. Next there is one unit on consonants and one unit on vowels. In these units, the sounds of English that often cause problems for nonnative speakers are presented with tips for pronunciation. It may be useful to skip around within these units, depending on individual needs.

These Pronunciation units also contain common words and dialogues with the difficult sounds of English. The dialogues are conversational and deal with campus life in a light-hearted way. They often generate discussions of slang and idioms, as well as campus culture.

Finally, the Pronunciation units provide space for individual word lists. ITAs or self-users are encouraged to list terminology from their own fields, or words from daily life that are difficult to pronounce. Then they can be more aware of these words and practice them regularly.

Discussions of Campus Culture

Appendix 1, "Discussions of Campus Culture," contains questions that provide a springboard for the discussion of many of the cultural issues at universities and colleges in the United States. Since most ITA trainers have their own approach to the discussion of U.S. culture, this is only a minor focus of this workbook. For a more comprehensive look at some of the issues of campus culture, another video program is recommended: *Encounters with Teaching,* by Jody Nyquist, Brooke Quigley, and Donald Wulff, available from the Center for Instructional Development and Research, University of Washington.

Transcripts

A major goal of the *Techniques for Teachers* program is to teach nonnative speakers of English to analyze American English speech. For this reason, the Transcripts in appendix 2 are a key element because they help nonnative speakers to understand extended pieces of natural speech in the context of the classroom. They may study the transcripts before, during, or after watching the video in order to analyze the way in which the U.S. teachers express themselves in an academic setting.

Most people will find that this supplementary material can be easily integrated with the rest of the *Techniques for Teachers* workbook. The Pronunciation sections can be covered gradually over a quarter or semester course, or used individually as needed. It is also easy to focus on specific English sounds during the Fluency Work activities in the main part of the workbook. Similarly, the Discussions of Campus Culture can be introduced as needed depending on the interests of the individual or group. Finally, the Transcripts of the videotape are a useful reference throughout the *Techniques for Teachers* program.

Part I

Lectures

Unit 1

Introductions

The first part of a class is called the introduction. An introduction serves several purposes. The first words may be a greeting or a call for students to pay attention. Most introductions also announce the main topic or activity of the class. Some teachers like to show a connection between previous material and any new material that will be covered. Others may mention the purpose or importance of the class: what the students are expected to learn. A detailed introduction may even give a step-by-step organizational plan for the class.

Teachers in Action

(*Play the videotape "Techniques for Teachers"*)

Videotape lessons 1-A, 1-B, and 1-C show examples of teachers giving introductions to lectures. As you watch the lessons, mark the chart to indicate the contents of each introduction.

Contents	1-A	1-B	1-C
Greeting	✓		
Announcements			
Review			✓
Call for Questions	✓		
Topic for Today	✓	✓	✓
Outline of Activities	✓	✓	
Purpose of Activities	✓		
Other			

Language Models

Listen to the three introductions a second time. Try to catch the phrases or sentences that the teachers use to get their points across. The first sentence is done for you.

1-A. Greeting   Hello, and welcome to the second class of Math 105.

      Questions _____

      Topic _____

1-B. Handout _____

      Topic _____

      Example _____

1-C. Review _____

      Topic _____

Study these phrases. Add the ones you like to your own vocabulary.

Speech Patterns: Sentence Stress

The English language has definite patterns of intonation, including stress, timing, and pitch. If you learn the intonation patterns of English, it will be easier for you to understand spoken English. It will also be easier for others to understand you, because the English listener follows the thread of a speaker's words by listening for intonation patterns.

In the Speech Patterns sections of this book you will find rules for the intonation patterns of English. The accompanying exercises help you listen for these patterns and bring them into your own speech.

English speakers use sentence stress to call attention to the most important word or words in each sentence or phrase. There are three main reasons to use sentence stress (note that the sentence stress is italicized in each case).

1. Main Idea: Stress the word that contains the main idea.

   Example: This is a *Mathematics* class.

2. New Information: Stress the word that contains the new information.

   Example: The Mathematics class meets at *1:30*.

3. Comparison and Contrast: Stress two words that stand in comparison or contrast to each other.

   Example: Did you say *1:30* or *2:30*?

There are three ways to indicate sentence stress.

1. Say the word more loudly than the other words in the sentence.
2. Raise the pitch of your voice as you say the word.
3. Make the word extra long.

Look at these sentences from the first introduction (lesson 1-A).

Last time, we covered the administrative *details* of the course.

We're *now* ready to *begin* our study of the differential calculus and we'll begin with today's topic, the *derivative*.

The word *last* is stressed because it tells the listeners that a review of the last class is coming. Thus, it contains the main idea of the phrase, and also stands in contrast to *now* in the next sentence.

The word *details* is stressed because it is the main idea of the sentence.

The word *now* is stressed because it stands in contrast to *last*.

Begin is stressed because it stands in contrast to what happened in the last class, an overview of the administrative details of the course.

Derivative is stressed because it is the new information for today's topic.

Remember, these are general rules. Different speakers may stress different words depending on how they are thinking in their own minds. For more information see Judy Gilbert, "Pronunciation and Listening Comprehension," in *Current Perspectives on Pronunciation,* ed. J. Morley (Washington, D.C.: TESOL, 1987).

Fluency Work 1: Using Native Speaker Patterns

What does it mean to say that someone is fluent in a language? Fluency is a combination of language skills such as a knowledge of vocabulary and grammar, clear pronunciation of sounds, smooth intonation patterns—all these things play a role. Finally, there is an emotional aspect to fluency. The more you can develop a comfortable feeling for speaking English, the more fluent you will become. These activities will improve your fluency through analyzing the language patterns used in lesson 1-B.

1. Listen to the tape and notice the *italicized* words. These are the words that have the most stress. Decide why the speaker stresses these words based on the rules for sentence stress. Of course, the answer may depend on how the speaker is thinking about her own words. Another person might stress it differently.
2. Circle the words that are difficult for you to pronounce.
3. Read the paragraph yourself. Try it several times while you also stress the main words, just like the speaker.

Lesson 1-B

We have a single page *handout* today which has 4 *graphs* on it that we'll be *talking* about during the course of today's *lecture*. The *topic* for today is the idea of *correlation*. We can *look* at the word correlation and see that it's really made up of *two parts*: "*co,*" meaning *together*. You've seen that part of a word in words like "*cooperation,*" "*co-workers.*" And "*relation.*" So we're gonna look at the *relation together* of *two* variables. We're gonna look at the *correlation* between two variables.

Fluency Work 2: Giving Introductions

These outlines contain information typically found in introductions. Present the information in your own words to a partner or to the class, using strong sentence stress for the most important words. You may wish to tape-record yourself after practicing.

Introductions 7

1. Yesterday: Chapter 7

    Today: Chapter 8

    Activities:

    a. Finding derivatives

    b. Page 67, problem set 4

2. Last week: Finished Chapter 11

    Today: Quiz—Chapter 11

    Activities:

    a. Review Chapter 11 (10 minutes)

    b. Quiz (20 minutes)

    c. Begin Chapter 12 (20 minutes)

3. Supply your own information from an imaginary class.

    Review:

    Today:

    Activities:

Fluency Work 3: Speech Analysis

By speaking freely on tape and then analyzing your own speech, you can learn a lot about the patterns of your language. Follow these steps in analyzing your own speech.

1. Plan an introduction to a class in your field. You may use Number 3 from the exercise above as an outline.

2. Tape-record the introduction in your own words; do not read a prepared speech.

3. Listen to the tape and carefully write down your exact words. This is called a transcription. (This takes a long time, but it gives you a text that you can analyze.)

4. Make improvements in the grammar, vocabulary, wording, or content if you need to.

5. Mark your transcription by <u>underlining</u> the stressed words.

6. Circle any words that are difficult to pronounce. Practice these difficult words.

7. Read the passage from your transcription and tape-record it again. Compare the first version to the new version.

8. Put away your transcription. Say the introduction in your own words and tape-record it. Compare this version to the other versions.

Miniclass Assignment

The purpose of the miniclass assignments in this book is to give you a chance to bring together all your skills in a short, simulated class. How you use these assignments depends on your situation. It is reasonable for three to five people to do miniclasses in an hour. If you are in a class with a larger number of people, you might decide to do miniclasses in small groups of four or five. People in the group can act as students for each other.

The Topic Ideas are designed for groups of people from different fields, so that the level of the miniclass will be simple enough for everyone to understand. If the whole class is from the same field, you may choose more complex topics.

Another way to use these assignments is to adapt them to a real class that you teach. You may want to place a tape recorder in your classroom and record the class so that you can later review what you did.

For this unit's assignment, teach a very simple concept to the class. Plan the introduction especially well, using ideas from the unit and these suggestions.

1. Spend 5 to 7 minutes.
2. Use notes or the board, but do not read a prepared speech.
3. Use strong sentence stress for the important words.
4. Plan your introduction carefully.
5. Use the Vocabulary Planner.
6. Video- or audiotape your miniclass.
7. Others in the class are the students for each teacher.

Topic Idea: Why This Field Is Important

Tell the class why your field is important. What are some of the famous discoveries in your field? What kind of research do people do now? What kinds of jobs do people get with a degree in your field?

Vocabulary Planner

List the specialized words and phrases you plan to use in your miniclass. Mark the stress patterns for each word or phrase. Circle any troublesome sounds. Practice pronouncing these words and phrases before you teach your miniclass.

Introductions

Word or Phrase   *Pronunciation Notes*

Self-Evaluation

If your miniclass was video- or audiotaped, watch or listen to the tape as you fill out this evaluation form.

1. What information did your introduction contain?

   Greeting

   Announcements

   Review

   Call for questions

   Topic for today

   Outline of activities

   Purpose of activities

   Other

2. How did you introduce each of the items on the list above? Write down the word or phrase that you used next to each item above.

3. What did the students learn from your miniclass? How do you know?

4. What changes would you make if you had to do this again?

5. List any questions about grammar, vocabulary, or pronunciation.

Trainer Feedback Guidelines

ITA trainers who wish to give feedback on miniclasses may want to follow these suggested guidelines. They may be applied to any of the Miniclass Assignments in this workbook.

1. Summarize what happened in the miniclass. Communicate what you observe in a nonjudgmental way.

2. Comment on the use of the specific skills covered in each unit.

3. Specify the strong points of the miniclass.

4. Recommend any changes that would improve the lesson. It is best to mention only those changes that the ITA is actually capable of making. Try not to overwhelm the person with criticism.

5. Note any language problems. Give pronunciation, grammar, and/or vocabulary tips.

Observation Assignment

Observe two classes on your university campus. You may observe the same instructor twice or observe two different instructors. Most instructors in large classrooms do not mind an extra observer as long as you ask permission first. If you are taking classes now, observe your own teachers.

Write down the following information for each class on a separate page.

1. Describe the introduction. What kind of information did the instructor give?

2. Were you able to tell when the introduction stopped and the body of the class began? How could you tell?

3. Did the content of the class fit the introduction?

4. List any useful phrases that you heard.

5. Which of the two introductions did you prefer? Why?

Unit 2

Transitions

The word *transition* means "change." In a classroom, a transition is a change from one topic or activity to another. For example, a teacher might introduce a formula, and then solve a problem with that formula. There should be a transition between these two activities:

Introduce the formula + Transition + Solve a problem.

As you move from one topic or activity to another in class, you will probably make many transitions, both large and small. The more clearly you make transitions, the easier it will be for the listeners to understand you and take notes.

There are five ways to make transitions.

Review

If you stop and quickly review what you have just said, the listeners will know that you are finished with that section.

Example (from lesson 2-A):

At this point we've completed our definition and given one example.

Call for Questions

A call for questions lets the students know that you are finished with a section.

Example (from lesson 2-A)

Before we move on to a more general interpretation of the derivative, are there any questions at this point?

Transition Words

Words or phrases such as "first," "second," "finally," and "on the other hand" help your listeners follow your lesson. These words are usually stressed.

Pause

If you pause, students will realize that you are about to move on to something new and feel free to ask questions.

Preview

A short statement about what will happen next prepares the students for a new topic or activity.

Example (from lesson 2-C)

Next, what I'd like to do is work a mathematical example.

Teachers in Action

(Play the videotape "Techniques for Teachers")

Lessons 2-A through 2-H show teachers making transitions in lecturing situations. As you watch the lessons, try to identify the different techniques the teachers use to make transitions. Fill in the chart by checking off the transition markers used in lessons 2-A through 2-F. The first one is completed for you.

	2-A	2-B	2-C	2-D	2-E	2-F
Review	x					
Call for questions	x					
Transition words	x					
Pause	x					
Preview						

Language Models

Lesson 2-G is rather long. In it, we see the teacher describing four plots on the board. Notice how easy it is to tell when the teacher moves from one plot to the next because of the transition words she uses. It is also clear by the way she herself moves and points to each part of the board.

Play lesson 2-G again. What phrases does the teacher use to move from one plot to the next? Which words does she emphasize the most? Fill in the blanks with the phrases the teacher uses in lesson 2-G.

Let's begin _____

(First plot) So refer _____

(Second plot) Let's skip _____

(Third plot) _____

(Fourth plot) Well, let's _____

Speech Patterns 1: Pauses

Fluent speakers divide their language up into small groups of thoughts as they speak. When we write, we can use commas and periods to signal the thought groups, but when we speak, we have to use pauses to show where each thought group begins and ends. It is natural to take in a breath during a pause.

Pauses also help the listener follow the logic of what the speaker says.

A rather technical passage with no punctuation follows. Decide where to put the pauses, using a slash (/) to mark each pause. Compare your analysis with others. Notice that the meaning changes depending on where the pause is.

The subjects were treated about 10 days later we analyzed them to discover the changes we had predicted that growth would occur unless the order of treatment was reversed was considered.

These are some situations in which pauses often occur.

1. Pause after a transition word such as *first, finally,* or *however.*

    First, / we are going to look at this chart.

2. Pause before and after an important word that you want to emphasize, keeping the article with the noun.

    And it measures / the strength / of correlation.

3. Pause between the sentences and sometimes between clauses.

    This chart is important. / It summarizes the chapter.

    This chart is important / because it summarizes the chapter.

4. In general, do not separate phrases. Pauses usually go after the content words (nouns, adverbs, adjectives, verbs), not after the structure words (prepositions, auxiliaries, pronouns, articles).

    (Lesson 2-G): The final plot for today / depicts prices of houses / in a particular small town.

Fluency Work 1: Pauses in Speech

The excerpt given below is from Lesson 2-G. Play the videotape and do the following activities.

1. Notice the slash (/) marks that show where there is a pause. Discuss how these pauses follow the rules above.
2. <u>Underline</u> the words that receive the most stress. Compare your analysis with others; you may find different opinions.
3. Circle the words that are difficult to pronounce.
4. Read the paragraph yourself. Try it several times following the pauses and stress of the native speaker.

Lesson 2-G

The third plot that we have / the one that's labeled / baseball / on the lower lefthand

corner of your handout / were collected / to investigate the question as to whether /

American league baseball teams / which are at higher altitudes / whose home parks are at higher altitudes / tend to score more home runs / um / the theory being / that if you're at a higher altitude / the air is thinner / and therefore the ball will go further / and so we have here / the 1972 figures / from the American league / and / if we stand back away from this plot / and look for its basic shape / well / we'd like to see it being nice and oval-shaped / but actually / I see it / being just a big / nebulous cloud of points / with no particular pattern to it.

Speech Patterns 2: Transition Words Chart

This chart shows some common transition words in English.

Meaning	Transition Word
New idea	First
	First of all
	Number one
	Now
	Okay
Additional idea	Second
	Third
	And
	Plus
	Also
	Another
	Next
	Then
	Finally
	Okay
	Now
	So
Cause	The reason is
	Because
	Since

Effect	So
	As a result
	Therefore
	Thus
	Consequently
Contrast	But
	And yet
	In contrast
	On the other hand
	However
	Whereas

Fluency Work 2: Using Transition Words

Use these outlines of announcements to practice making transitions from one idea to the next. Using transition words, present the information in each outline in your own words to the class. Remember to put a strong emphasis on transition words and to pause between thought groups.

1. Homework:

    Read pages 23–36

    Do exercises 1–6

    Skip exercise 5

    Study the chart—page 37

    Due Friday, this week

2. Midterm Exam:

    Date:

    Time:

    Bring: calculator
    scratch paper
    sharp pencil

    Don't bring notes or books

    Work quickly

    Don't miss it!

3. Tips to study for the Midterm Exam—Please review:

    Chapters 1–6 in textbook

    All lecture notes

Quizzes

Homework problems

This week's lectures not included

4. Special study session—to prepare for the Midterm

Time:

Date:

Bring questions on confusing points

It is not required; voluntary

5. Make up your own announcements.

Speech Patterns 3: Comparison and Contrast

To compare is to look at how one thing is similar to another. To contrast is to look at how one thing is different from another. In lesson 2-G, June compares and contrasts the four graphs on the board. She uses three important language techniques to do this.

1. She uses transition words that show comparison or contrast.

    Example:

    So <u>whereas</u> we saw with the ducks and with the demographics that if I told you something about the value of the variable that was on the horizontal axis, you could probably tell me something about the value of the variable on the vertical axis, <u>whereas</u> for the baseball set of data, knowing the altitude of the ball park really doesn't tell me very much about how many homeruns I would have expected from that particular team.

2. She uses parallel word order. This tells the listener that she is making a similar point about two different things.

    Examples:

    Smaller values correspond to being more like a mallard; larger values correspond to being more like a pintail.

    ...ducks that had a higher plumage rating tended also to have a higher behavioral rating; ducks that had a lower plumage rating tended also to have a lower behavioral rating.

3. She stresses the words that stand in comparison or contrast to each other.

    Example:

    Definitely. When we have higher values of square <u>footage</u>, we also have higher values of <u>price</u>.

Which words does June stress in the examples in 1 and 2 above?
Note that prefixes may show contrast. Stress the prefix itself in that case.

Examples: der<u>i</u>vative   <u>an</u>tiderivative

   adv<u>an</u>tage   <u>dis</u>advantage

   <u>na</u>tural   <u>un</u>natural

Fluency Work 3: Comparing and Contrasting Information

Use the information in these outlines to make comparisons and contrasts. Use your own words. Try these ideas:

Use transition words if appropriate.

Use parallel structure.

Stress the words that stand in comparison or contrast to each other.

Look at the example.

   Read—foreign language—easy
   Speak—foreign language—difficult

   I think that <u>reading</u> a foreign language is <u>easy,</u> but I think that <u>speaking</u> a foreign language is <u>difficult</u>.

   1. Advantage of used car—cheaper
      Advantage of new car—better quality

   2. Advantage of used car—cheaper
      Disadvantge of used car—lower quality

   3. 1980—Reagan—U.S. president
      1984—Reagan—U.S. president
      1988—Bush—U.S. president

   4. x positive—function increasing
      x negative—function decreasing

   5. 20% students—live with parents
      45% students—live in student housing
      35% students—live in apartments or houses

   6. Advantage of dorm—location
      Disadvantage—noise

   7. This quarter—course work
      Next quarter—dissertation work

8. My rent due—1st of month
   Payday—5th of month!

9. Humanities departments—financial problems
   Science departments—more funding
   Engineering departments—rolling in money!

Make up your own comparisons and contrasts:

10.

11.

12.

Fluency Work 4: Speech Analysis

By speaking freely on tape and then analyzing your own speech, you can learn more about the patterns of your language. Follow these steps in analyzing your own speech.

1. Plan to make several announcements, using transitions to connect them. You may use number 5 from page 19.

2. Tape-record the announcements in your own words; do not read a prepared speech.

3. Listen to the tape and carefully write down (transcribe) your exact words.

4. Make improvements in the grammar, vocabulary, wording, or content if you need to.

5. Mark your transcription to show which words are stressed and where the pauses belong. Underline the stressed words and mark pauses with a slash (/).

6. Circle any words that are difficult to pronounce. Practice these difficult words.

7. Read the passage from your transcription and tape-record it again. Compare the first version to the new version.

8. Put away your transcription. Give the announcements again in your own words and tape-record them. Compare this version to the other versions.

Miniclass Assignment

Teach two related concepts to the class. Choose very simple concepts from your field. Make a clear transition between the first concept and the second concept, following these suggestions.

1. Spend 5 to 7 minutes.
2. Use notes or the board, but do not read or memorize a prepared speech.
3. Use stress and pauses to emphasize your transitions.
4. Use the Vocabulary Planner.
5. Video- or audiotape your miniclass.

Topic Idea: The Metric System

Introduce the metric system (U.S. students may not be familiar with it). Talk about two different parameters: length and mass. Be sure to use a transition when you move from the idea of length to the idea of mass.

Vocabulary Planner

List the specialized words and phrases you plan to use in your miniclass. Mark the stress patterns for each word or phrase. Circle any troublesome sounds. Practice pronouncing these important words and phrases before you teach your miniclass.

Word or Phrase   *Pronunciation Notes*

Self-Evaluation

If your miniclass was video- or audiotaped, watch or listen to the tape as you fill out this self-evaluation form.

1. What main concepts did you present?

    a.

    b.

    c. (others?)

2. What technique(s) did you use to mark the transitions?

    a. Review

    b. Preview

    c. Pause

    d. Call for questions

    e. Transition words (which ones?)

3. What changes would you make if you had to do this miniclass again?

4. List any questions about grammar, vocabulary, or pronunciation.

Unit 3
Restating and Summarizing

To restate something means to say it again. A good way to emphasize an important point in a class is to restate or repeat the point more than once. In fact, a good rule of thumb is that if a point is really important, you should tell the listeners what you are going to say, say it, and then repeat what you have just said. You may repeat the point with exactly the same words, or you may rephrase your statement using different words. By writing the point on the board, you can also emphasize its importance.

A summary is a review of main ideas. Some classes end with a summary, and others begin with a summary of the previous class. Many teachers use a summary when they finish a section of their class. A simple review of the main points covered helps students organize and check their notes. It also tells students that it is time to move on to a new topic.

Teachers in Action

(Play the videotape "Techniques for Teachers")

Lessons 3-A through 3-E show examples of teachers using restatement to emphasize an important point. As you watch the lessons, try to identify the important point that is restated and write it down. The first one is completed for you.

    3-A. The derivative is the rate of change.

    3-B. (Later in the same lecture):

    3-C. (Later in the same lecture):

    3-D.

    3-E.

Lessons 3-F through 3-H show examples of a teacher using a short summary to make a transition from one part of the class to the next. In each case, what information is included in the summary? Notice which verb tense is used in the summaries. Why is this tense used?

    3-F. Information:

        Verb tense:

    3-G. Information:

        Verb tense:

    3-H. Information:

        Verb tense:

Lessons 3-I and 3-J show conclusions in which the teachers summarize the main points of the class. In each case, write down the phrase they use to introduce their summaries.

    3-I. Phrase:

    3-J. Phrase:

Language Models

Study these excerpts from the videotape lessons carefully. Add the ones you like to your own vocabulary.

Restatements

3-A. That concept is important so let me write it down for you and say it again.

3-B. ...the fact is, the slope of the tangent line is the same as the derivative. That's an important idea. The slope of this tangent line equals the derivative of $f(x)$.

3-C. Remember what a derivative is; it's the rate of change.

3-D. The correlation coefficient in standard notation is denoted lower case r, and it measures the linear relationship between two variables, so the correlation coefficient measures the strength of a linear relationship between two variables.

3-E. And the most important thing to think about is, what is the consumer willing to pay for? That's really the underlying question: what are they willing to pay for? So, not only what need does it satisfy, but what are they willing to pay for?

Summaries

3-F. So far, we have given a formal definition and shown some of the intuition behind it.

3-G. So we've actually computed an example of a derivative from first principles, and verified from drawing a picture that it makes intuitive sense.

3-H. So, so far, we've looked at four plots.

3-I. Let me summarize what we've done today.

3-J. So let's step back and look at what we've talked about.

Fluency Work 1: Using Native Speaker Patterns

The excerpt given below is from lesson 3-A. Play the videotape and do the following activities.

1. Underline the words that receive the most stress. Compare your analysis with others and discuss any differences.

2. Mark a slash (/) to show where there is a pause. Compare your slashes with others in the class and discuss any differences.

3. Circle the words that are difficult to pronounce.

4. Read the paragraph yourself. Try it several times following the pauses and stress of the native speaker.

Lesson 3-A

That derivative is defined as notation f prime of x equals, the limit, as an auxiliary variable that's just in there temporarily, goes to zero, of the ratio of how much f changes, that's f of (x plus h) minus f of x, with respect to how much x itself is changed by moving from x to (x plus h). That ratio, in the limit, for very very small h, that gives us the instantaneous rate of change, defines the derivative. That concept is important so let me write it down for you and say it again; this derivative gives us the instantaneous rate of change of the function f with respect to the variable letter x.

Fluency Work 2: Making Restatements

Use these outlines to make important announcements to the class or to a partner, using your own words. Restate the announcements because they are so important.

1. Room change:

    Starting Friday

    Class in Lewis Hall 107

    Not in Ross Hall 305

2. Date of Midterm Exam:

    Place:

    Time:

    (Choose any date, place, and time)

3. Field trip to the observatory:

    Bus leaves Friday, 8:30 P.M., in front of the library

4. Department picnic:

   Saturday, July 20, Laurelhurst Beach

   12:00, noon

   Bring a salad and drink (department supplies barbeque)

   Family and friends welcome

5. New rule:

   No more eating in class.

   It's too messy.

   Other teachers have complained.

6. Make up your own announcements:

   a.

   b.

   c.

Fluency Work 3: Giving a Summary

Find an interesting article from your campus newspaper or a city newspaper and read the article carefully. <u>Underline</u> the important words. Bring the article to class to practice summaries. Try these activities.

1. *Detailed summary.* Summarize the article for the class or for a partner. Use your own words, but include some of the key words that you underlined in advance. Your summary will be shorter than the article, but it should still include all the main points.

2. *Brief summary.* Summarize only the most important points of the article. Try to do this in one or two sentences.

3. *Summary of a summary.* Have another class member summarize your brief summary in his or her own words. This will help you know whether your own summary was understandable.

Fluency Work 4: Speech Analysis

By speaking freely on tape and then analyzing your own speech, you can learn more about the patterns of your language. Follow these steps in analyzing your own speech.

1. Plan to make an announcement, using restatement to emphasize it. You may use Number 6 from Fluency Work 2.

2. Tape-record the announcement in your own words; do not read a prepared speech.

3. Listen to the tape and carefully transcribe your exact words.

4. Make improvements in the grammar, vocabulary, wording, or content if you need to.

5. Mark your transcription to show which words are stressed and where the pauses belong. <u>Underline</u> the stressed words and mark the pauses with slashes (/).

6. Circle any words that are difficult to pronounce. Practice these difficult words.

7. Read the passage from your transcription and tape-record it again. Compare the first version to the new version.

8. Put away your transcription. Give the announcement again in your own words and tape-record it. Compare this version to the other versions.

Miniclass Assignment

Present a simple concept to the class. Use restatements in the body of your miniclass to make your main points clear. At the end, summarize your class. Follow these suggestions.

1. Spend 5 to 7 minutes.

2. Use the board. You may wish to write your main points as well as restate them.

3. Use the Vocabulary Planner.

4. Video- or audiotape your miniclass.

Topic Idea: Book Review

Choose a fundamental book in your field. Tell the class the author and title and briefly explain the book's contents. Why is it such an important book? Restate the author and title of the book and write them on the board. Finally, restate the important points of the book.

Vocabulary Planner

List the specialized words and phrases you plan to use in your miniclass. Mark the stress patterns for each word or phrase. Circle any troublesome sounds. Practice pronouncing these important words and phrases before you teach your miniclass.

Restating and Summarizing

Word or Phrase　　　　　　　　　*Pronunciation Notes*

Self-Evaluation

If your miniclass was video- or audiotaped, watch or listen to the tape as you fill out this evaluation form.

1. Which main points of this lesson did you restate?

2. Did you summarize at the end?

3. Do you think this use of restatement and summary helped the listeners understand?

4. Write down the phrases you used to introduce
   a. Restatements

   b. Summary

5. What changes would you make if you had to do this miniclass again?

6. List any questions about grammar, vocabulary, or pronunciation.

Unit 4

Definitions

Every field has its own special terminology, and one of the purposes of an introductory course is to teach that terminology to students. Therefore, definitions of terms occur frequently in introductory courses.

Definitions may be very simple. Sometimes just a synonym of the term or a short explanatory phrase will do the job. In technical fields, a definition may be a formula. Definitions in some fields require certain special words or "jargon." It should be easy to find the correct wording for a definition in an introductory textbook for a given field. Learn the conventional jargon of the definition, but also be prepared to explain the meaning of that jargon.

Teachers in Action

(Play the videotape "Techniques for Teachers")

Lessons 4-A through 4-G show teachers using definitions. In each case, write down the term that is being defined.

4-A. Term:

4-B. Term:

4-C. Term:

4-D. Term:

4-E. Term:

4-F. Term:

4-G. Term:

Speech Patterns 1: Using Pauses to Emphasize a Word

When you introduce a new term, you will probably want to emphasize that term so that everyone hears it clearly and pays attention to the meaning. Unit 1 mentions three ways to stress a word.

1. Say the word more loudly than the other words.

2. Raise the pitch of your voice as you say the word.

3. Make the stressed syllable of the word extra long.

This is a fourth way to emphasize a word or term.

4. Pause and take in a breath before and after the term.

(Note: if the term is a noun and it has an article before it, put the article after the first pause, with the noun.)

Notice the pauses in this example from lesson 4-E. Because the term *correlation coefficient* has two words, the teacher pauses before and after each word for a very strong emphasis, (the slashes [/] mark the pauses).

It's called / the correlation / coefficient / and it measures the strength of correlation.

Also notice that the article *the* stays with the word *correlation*.

Speech Patterns 2: Using Pauses in a Definition

If a definition is a synonym or simple sentence, you can use pauses to indicate that you are giving the definition. Pause before and after the definition, like this.

Term + Pause + (or) + Definition + Pause + Rest of sentence.
                 (so)
                 (that is)
                 (meaning)

Study these examples from the tape and read them out loud.

4-A. And the question that was being addressed is whether crossbreeds / so ducks that have one mallard parent and one pintail parent / if you look at them. . . .

    Term   = Crossbreeds

    Definition = Ducks that have one mallard parent and one pintail parent

4-C. It's that marginal cost / the cost of producing one more unit / that we are interested in.

    Term   = Marginal cost

    Definition = The cost of producing one more unit

4-D. . . . it's really made up of two parts: / "co" / meaning "together," / and "relation."

    Term   = "Co"

    Definition = Together

Language Models

These definitions are from lessons 4-A through 4-G. Study them carefully. Add the phrasing you like to your own vocabulary.

4-A. . . . crossbreeds, so ducks that have one mallard parent and one pintail parent, if you look at them. . . .

4-B. The exact definition of this derivative is as follows.

4-C. There's something that economists call a marginal cost. That's defined as the extra cost of producing one more object in a factory. . . .

4-D. We can look at the word *correlation* and see that it's really made up of two parts: *co,* meaning together, and relation.

4-E. ... and we do, as statisticians, have a statistic: it's called the correlation coefficient ... and it measures the strength of a linear relationship between two variables.

4-F. When ... we notice that we have basically an oval-shaped scatter diagram pointing upwards, we say that the scatter diagram is depicting positive correlation.

4-G. (Functional features: do you mean additional features to the bike?) A feature that affects the way it's used, yeah, the way it functions.

Fluency Work 1: Using Native Speaker Patterns

The excerpt given below is from lesson 4-F. Play the videotape again while you do the following activities.

1. Underline the words which receive the most stress and mark the pauses with slashes (/).
2. Circle the words that are difficult to pronounce.
3. Read the paragraph yourself. Try it several times following the pauses and stress of the native speaker.

Lesson 4-F

When we look at plots and we notice that we have basically an oval-shaped scatter diagram pointing upwards we say that the scatter diagram is depicting positive correlation. So here we've got positive correlation or we can say that the two variables, plumage and behavior, are positively correlated. If the scatter diagram is pointing downwards, then we've got negative correlation and if we're in the third case and we have a round, nebulous cloud of points with no clear orientation, pretty much what we can say about the correlation is that there is very little or perhaps no correlation.

Speech Patterns 3: Word Stress

Any English word of two or more syllables has a specific stress pattern. There is always one syllable that carries the main stress of the word; there may also be another syllable that carries a secondary stress. When you learn a new word, learn the stress pattern too. If you pronounce the word with the stress on the wrong syllable, the listener may not understand the word.

Remember the three ways to stress a syllable.

1. Raise the pitch of your voice.
2. Make the syllable louder.
3. Make the syllable longer.

Unstressed vowels are often reduced in long English words. "Reduced" means that they are pronounced like ə, (a neutral sound called *schwa*).

For example: Possíbility (5 syllables, stress on the 3d)
                     ə   ə

This word has three *i*'s in it. The middle one is stressed, so it is pronounced clearly. The other two are not stressed and are pronounced like ə.

If you do not reduce these vowels, listeners may think that you are putting stress on them. They may not catch the word at all.

Say the following words out loud. Decide which vowels should be reduced and notice how the reduced vowels shift when the words change form.

geography	geographical	confer	conference
biology	biological	rigid	rigidity
economy	economic	mystery	mysterious
photography	photograph	victory	victorious
abolish	abolition	hypothesis	hypothetical
confirm	confirmation	parallel	parallelogram

However, note that unstressed vowels are not *always* reduced. In these words, the vowels are not reduced.

| rewrite | multimedia | forty | matriarchy |

Speech Patterns 4: Longer Terminology

Some of the terminology in your field may consist of more than one word. Each of the words in the term has its own stress pattern, but, in addition to that, one word has a stronger stress than the others. Here are two simple rules for the pronunciation of two-word terms.

1. In an adjective + noun combination, the noun usually has more stress.

    Examples: formal definition
    final exam
    electrical engineering
    mass media
    hazardous waste

2. In a noun + noun combination, the first noun usually has more stress.

    Examples: office hour
    math department
    x-axis
    correlation coefficient
    set theory
    field trip
    stock market

Fluency Work 2: Giving Definitions

Write down five basic terms from your field. Choose terms that every new student must learn in your field. For each term, do these activities.

1. Make sure you can pronounce the term correctly. How many syllables are there? Which one takes the stress? Are there any reduced vowels? If a term consists of more than one word, which word gets the most stress? Mark the stress pattern above the term. Practice saying the term clearly.

2. Write a definition of the term using simple words.

3. Put your list away. Use your own words to give each of your definitions to a classmate. Explain the meanings clearly in simple language.

Term 1. (mark the stress)

    Simple definition:

Term 2: (mark the stress)

    Simple definition:

Term 3: (mark the stress)

    Simple definition:

Term 4: (mark the stress)

    Simple definition:

Term 5: (mark the stress)

    Simple definition:

Fluency Work 3: Speech Analysis

By speaking freely on tape and then analyzing your own speech, you can learn a lot about the patterns of your language. Follow these steps in analyzing your own speech.

1. Plan to give three short definitions. You may use some of the terms you listed in the previous activity.

2. Tape-record the definitions in your own words; do not read a prepared speech.

3. Listen to the tape and carefully transcribe your exact words.

4. Make improvements in the grammar, vocabulary, wording, or content if you need to.

5. Mark your transcription to show which words are stressed and where the pauses belong. Underline the stressed words and mark the pauses with slashes (/).

6. Circle any words that are difficult to pronounce. Practice these difficult words.

7. Read the passage from your transcription and tape-record it again. Compare the first version to the new version.

8. Put away your transcription. Give the definitions again in your own words and tape-record them. Compare this version to the other versions.

Miniclass Assignment

Present two basic definitions to the class (you may use definitions from the previous activity). If your definitions include jargon, be prepared to explain what that jargon means. Follow these suggestions.

1. Spend 5 to 7 minutes.

2. Use simple language.

3. Make a clear transition between the two definitions.

4. Use the Vocabulary Planner.

5. Video- or audiotape your presentation.

Vocabulary Planner

List the specialized words and phrases you plan to use in your miniclass. Mark the stress patterns for each word or phrase. Circle any troublesome sounds. Practice pronouncing these important words and phrases before you teach your miniclass.

Word or Phrase   *Pronunciation Notes*

Self-Evaluation

If your miniclass was video- or audiotaped, watch or listen to the tape as you fill out this evaluation form.

1. Which terms did you define?

    a.

    b.

2. What information did you include in your definitions?

    a.

    b.

3. Which definition was clearest, in your opinion? Why?

4. What changes would you make if you had to do this miniclass again?

5. List any questions about grammar, vocabulary, or pronunciation.

Unit 5

Examples

Everyone is familiar with examples; they are very common in both the classroom and daily conversation as well. By using an example, you can make your meaning clear to listeners. Teachers often use examples to make abstract material more concrete. By drawing on students' previous knowledge from daily life or from material presented earlier in the course, the teacher can help students see a simpler, more concrete picture of a difficult concept.

Teachers in Action

(Play the videotape "Techniques for Teachers")

Lessons 5-A through 5-E show teachers using examples from daily life. While you watch each lesson, write down: what the example is, what concept is being explained by the example, and what the teacher assumes that students know. The first one is completed for you.

> 5-A. Concept: The derivative.
>
> > Example: A car is driving at different speeds from Seattle.
> > Students know: A person can drive a car at different speeds.
>
> 5-B. Concept (later in the same lecture):
>
> > Example:
> >
> > Students know:
>
> 5-C. Concept (later in the same lecture):
>
> > Example:
> >
> > Students know:
>
> 5-D. Concept:
>
> > Example:
> >
> > Students know:
>
> 5-E. Concept:
>
> > Example:
> >
> > Students know: A Cuisinart is a brand of food processor, an appliance that chops food. It is rather large.

Language Models

These passages are used to introduce examples in the videotape lessons. Study them carefully and add the ones you like to your own vocabulary.

> 5-A. For example, let the function f represent the distance from Seattle at time x.
>
> 5-A. Let's suppose you start off initially in Seattle.
>
> 5-B. The next is from vocabulary. If you imagine children learning words over time and you let the function $f(x)$ represent the number of words that they know at age x....

5-C. I have one more specific example for you today. This example is from physics, and concerns how fast an object falls when you drop it—for example, an eraser to the floor.

5-E. I think that one thing that you see often in examples like Japan, if they're trying to sell kitchen appliances, for example....

Additional Phrases to Introduce Examples

For instance	Take the case of
Suppose	Let's say
Supposing	Consider

Fluency Work 1: Using Native Speaker Patterns

The excerpt given below is from lesson 5-E. Play the videotape again and do the following activities.

1. Underline the words that receive the most stress and mark the pauses with slashes (/).
2. Circle the words that are difficult to pronounce.
3. Read the paragraph yourself. Try it several times following the stress and pauses of the native speaker.

Lesson 5-E

Well, I think that one thing you see often in examples like Japan, if they're trying to sell kitchen appliances, for example, they might have done a little research to find out what need it satisfied. A food processor, Cuisinart would do really well if you think about how much chopping is involved in Japanese cooking, but the other thing you have to consider is what are they willing to pay for and if you have a very small kitchen, do you really want a Cuisinart when you could just have a knife? So, yeah, that's been a problem.

Fluency Work 2: Giving Examples

These sentences are statements of fact. Think of an example to make each fact clear, then, in your own words, state the fact and give the example. Be sure to introduce the example clearly. Work with a partner. The first one is completed for you.

1. Water is necessary to support life, but water can also be a destructive force.

   Example: For example, a flood can ruin a farmer's crops.

2. The type of food that you consider delicious may depend on what country you come from.

   Example:

3. Some scientists say that by the year 2020, the IQ of a computer will be equal to the IQ of a human. This will affect us in many ways.

   Example:

4. It is easy to see that synthetic materials, such as plastic, have changed our lives.

   Example:

5. It is very common to find symmetry in nature.

   Example:

6. (My field) is important to our daily lives.

   Example:

7. Oil prices are important to the world economy.

   Example:

8. (My field) has changed a lot in the last five years.

   Example:

9. It seems that every country has environmental problems of some kind.

   Example:

10. Air is necessary because we have to breathe it in order to survive, but it has other important functions too.

   Example:

Now, think of a simple fact from your field and find an example from daily life to make that fact clear. State your fact and example to a partner or to the class.

11. Fact:

   Example:

Fluency Work 3: Examples in Conversation

Examples are not used only in the classroom. We use them in conversation, too. In small groups or as a class, use examples to make conversation on these or other topics.

1. When you travel to North America from another country, you may find some customs that seem unusual to you. Give examples of customs that seem different or humorous.

2. Give examples of customs that travelers from North America might find unusual in your culture.

3. Give examples of fun and interesting ways to entertain out-of-town guests in this area.

Fluency Work 4: Speech Analysis

By speaking freely on tape and then analyzing your own speech, you can learn more about the patterns of your language. Follow these steps in analyzing your own speech.

1. Plan an example from your field.

2. Tape record the example in your own words; do not read a prepared speech.

3. Listen to the tape and carefully transcribe your exact words.

4. Make improvements in the grammar, vocabulary, wording, or content if you need to.

5. Mark your transcription to show which words are stressed and where the pauses belong. Underline the stressed words and mark the pauses with slashes (/).

6. Circle any words that are difficult to pronounce. Practice these difficult words.

7. Read the passage from your transcription and tape-record it again. Compare the first version to the new version.

8. Put away your transcription. Give the example again in your own words and tape-record it. Compare this version to the other versions.

Miniclass Assignment

Choose a simple concept from your field and teach it to the class. Include two examples in your lesson and follow these suggestions.

1. Spend 5 to 7 minutes.
2. Try to find examples from daily life.
3. Introduce your examples clearly.
4. Use the Vocabulary Planner.
5. Video- or audiotape your miniclass.

Topic Idea: My Field in the Future

Make some predictions for the class about where your field is heading in the future. Give examples of future areas of research and future jobs in your field.

Vocabulary Planner

List the specialized words and phrases you plan to use in your miniclass. Mark the stress patterns for each word or phrase. Circle any troublesome sounds. Practice pronouncing these important words and phrases before you teach your miniclass.

Word or Phrase   *Pronunciation Notes*

Word or Phrase   *Pronunciation Notes*

Self-Evaluation

If your miniclass was video- or audiotaped, watch or listen to the tape as you fill out this evaluation form.

1. What examples did you use?

    a.

    b.

    c. (others)

2. Write down the phrases you used to introduce your examples.

    a.

    b.

    c. (others)

3. Which example do you think the students understood most easily? Why?

4. What changes would you make if you had to do this miniclass again?

5. List any questions about grammar, vocabulary, or pronunciation.

Unit 6

Graphs and Diagrams

Before you begin the videotaped lessons for unit 6, review visual aids. There are many uses for graphs, diagrams, tables, and other "visuals" in the classroom. Often, a picture makes a point much more clearly than words. Several examples of different types of graphs, diagrams, and other visual aids are discussed below.

Line Graph

This graph tells us how many people used public transportation between cities in the United States between 1960 and 1980. The x-axis represents the time in years. The y-axis shows the number of millions of people who used transportation. Lines are drawn across the middle of the graph to show the difference between bus, train, and air transportation.

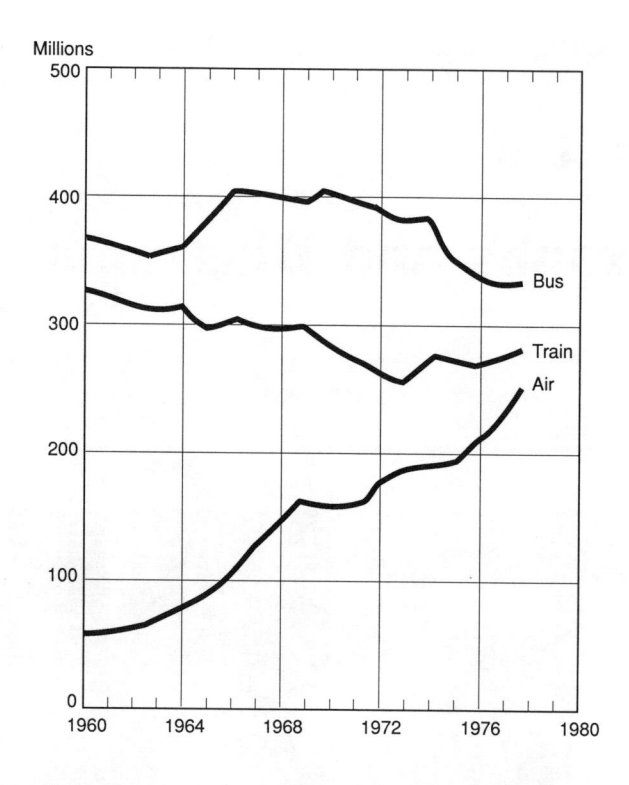

Comprehension Questions

1. Which type of transportation was used the most between 1960 and 1980?
2. Which type of transportation increased the most in use?
3. How many people use the train in 1973?

Important Vocabulary

x-axis	slope	rising	straight line
y-axis	steep	falling	diagonal line
point	gradual	quadrant	tangent line
line	maximum	coordinate	data
curve	minimum	symmetrical	function
plot	value	asymmetrical	represents

Bar Graph

This graph gives us information on how people voted for president in the U.S. elections in the recent past. Across the bottom of the graph we see a range of dates of elections

---

Source: U.S. Department of Commerce, Bureau of the Census, *Social Indicators III* (Washington, D.C.: GPO, 1980), 171.

from 1956 to 1984. The vertical bars on the graph show how many millions of votes there were. The white bars show Democratic votes; the gray bars show Republican votes; and the hatched bars show other candidates. It is easy to compare the numbers because the bars are lined up side by side.

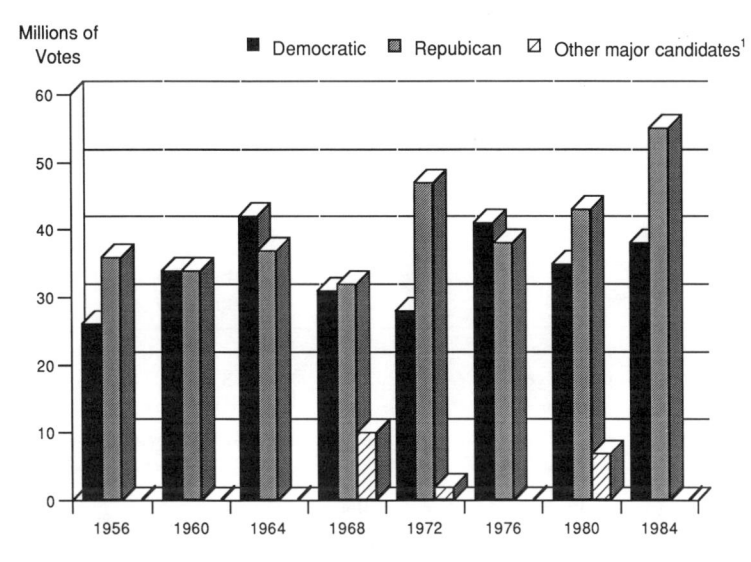

[1] 1968 and 1972—American Independent; 1980—John Anderson

Comprehension Questions

1. In which years did the Democratic candidate win the election?

2. What happened in 1960?

3. In which years did an outside candidate earn a significant number of votes?

Important Vocabulary

percent	hatching	vertical	longer	longest
bars	hatched	horizontal	shorter	shortest
data				

Table

This table also shows information about votes cast for president in the United States. Tables have vertical columns and horizontal rows. Each column contains one category of infor-

---

Source: U.S. Department of Commerce, Bureau of the Census, *Statistical Abstract of the United States* (Washington D.C.: GPO, 1988), 230.

mation. At the top of each column is a heading or subheading that tells what kind of information is in the column. For example, under the heading Candidates for President are two subheadings, Democratic and Republican. In the column below Democratic are the names of all the people who ran for president for the Democratic Party over the years. Likewise, in the column below the subheading marked Republican are the names of all the people who ran for president in the Republican Party. In this table you can also see statistics about how many votes were cast in each case.

	CANDIDATES FOR PRESIDENT		VOTE CAST FOR PRESIDENT					
			Total popular vote (1,000)	Democratic			Republican	
				Popular vote			Popular vote	
YEAR	Democratic	Republican		Number (1,000)	Percent	Electoral vote	Number (1,000)	Percent	Electoral vote
1920	Cox	Harding	26,768	9,133	34.1	127	16,153	60.3	404
1924	Davis	Coolidge	29,095	8,387	28.8	136	15,720	54.0	382
1928	Smith	Hoover	36,806	15,008	40.8	87	21,437	58.2	444
1932	F. D. Roosevelt	Hoover	39,758	22,829	57.4	472	15,760	39.6	59
1936	F. D. Roosevelt	Landon	45,654	27,757	60.8	523	16,684	36.5	8
1940	F. D. Roosevelt	Willkie	49,900	27,313	54.7	449	22,348	44.8	82
1944	F. D. Roosevelt	Dewey	47,977	25,613	53.4	432	22,018	45.9	99
1948	Truman	Dewey	48,794	24,179	49.6	303	21,991	45.1	189
1952	Stevenson	Eisenhower	61,551	27,315	44.4	89	33,936	55.1	442
1956	Stevenson	Eisenhower	62,027	26,023	42.0	73	35,590	57.4	457
1960	Kennedy	Nixon	68,838	34,227	49.7	303	34,108	49.5	219
1964	Johnson	Goldwater	70,645	43,130	61.1	486	27,178	38.5	52
1968	Humphrey	Nixon	73,212	31,275	42.7	191	31,785	43.4	301
1972	McGovern	Nixon	77,719	29,170	37.5	17	47,170	60.7	520
1976	Carter	Ford	81,556	40,831	50.1	297	39,148	48.0	240
1980	Carter	Reagan	86,515	35,484	41.0	49	43,904	50.7	489
1984	Mondale	Reagan	92,653	37,577	40.6	13	54,455	58.8	525

Source: U.S. Department of Commerce, Bureau of the Census, *Statistical Abstract of the United States* (Washington, D.C.: GPO, 1988), 232.

Comprehension Questions

1. In 1952, who ran for president and who won?

2. What percentage of the vote was Republican in 1960?

3. In which year was the total popular vote the greatest?

Graphs and Diagrams

Important Vocabulary

percent	column	heading	vertical
total	row	subheading	horizontal
statistics	data		

Pie Chart

A pie chart is round like a pie. It is most useful for showing data expressed in percentages because it is natural to think of a full circle as 100 percent. These pie charts show U.S. government income and expenditures estimated for 1989. The slices of the pie show what percentage of the total income is received from each different source or the percentage of government spending devoted to different programs.

The Federal Government Dollar, Fiscal Year 1989 Estimate

Where It Comes From . . .

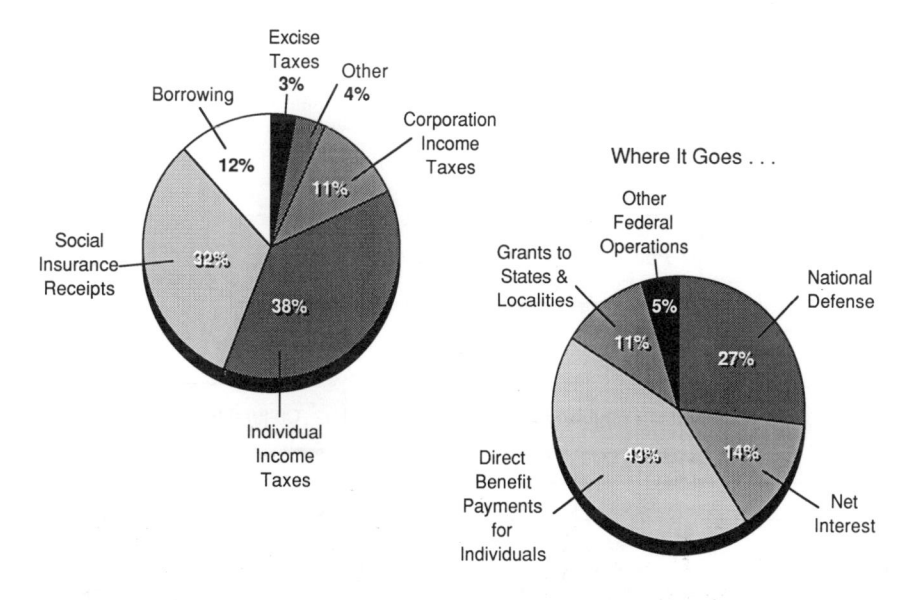

- Excise Taxes 3%
- Other 4%
- Borrowing 12%
- Corporation Income Taxes 11%
- Social Insurance Receipts 32%
- Individual Income Taxes 38%

Where It Goes . . .

- Other Federal Operations 5%
- Grants to States & Localities 11%
- National Defense 27%
- Net Interest 14%
- Direct Benefit Payments for Individuals 43%

Source: Executive Office of the President, Office of Management and Budget, *The United States Budget in Brief: Fiscal Year 1989* (Washington, D.C.: GPO, 1989), inside front cover.

Comprehension Questions

1. What percentage of U.S. income comes from borrowing?

2. What percentage does the United States spend on defense?

Important Vocabulary

slice	small part	large part	percentage
part	narrow slice	big slice	
piece	tiny piece	huge piece	

Tree Diagram

A tree diagram has branching parts just like a tree. It is used to show information that has a hierarchical or ordered relationship. This tree diagram is similar to the one on the blackboard in the "Techniques for Teachers" videotape, lesson 6-D. The teacher wants to show different factors that influence overseas trade. She decides to use a tree diagram to show that some factors are dependent on others.

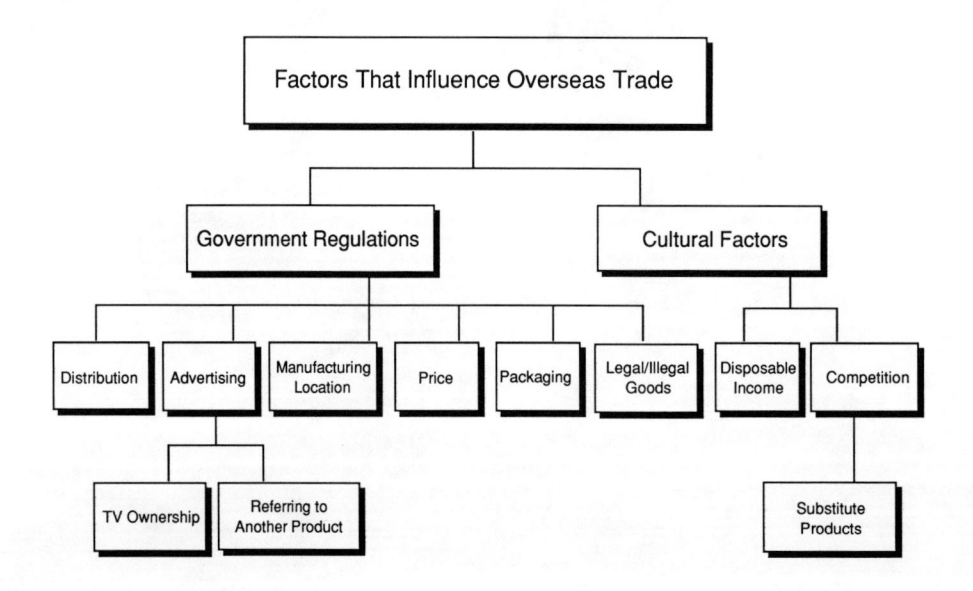

Graphs and Diagrams

Comprehension Questions

1. What are the two main subcategories that influence trade?

2. Which factors are subordinate to advertising?

3. If you wanted to add a new node to this diagram, "traditional style," where would you put it?

Important Vocabulary

hierarchy	branch	superior to	above
hierarchical relationship	branching	subordinate to	below
category	subcategory	dominated by	within
set	subset	node	

Other Visual Aids

There are many other types of visual materials to use in class. This is a list of possibilities.

drawings	maps
photographs	models
slides	diagrams of your own design
movies	

What all of these have in common is that they give students a more concrete picture of abstract material. Perhaps they offer students a different way of looking at the course material. Can you think of any other visual aids?

Teachers in Action

(Play the videotape "Techniques for Teachers")

Lessons 6-A through 6-D show four uses of graphs and diagrams. While you watch, describe the graph or diagram that you see, and tell what purpose it serves.

    6-A. Type of graph:

        Purpose:

6-B. Type of graph:

   Purpose:

6-C. Type of graph:

   Purpose:

6-D. Type of graph:

   Purpose:

Fluency Work 1: Using Native Speaker Patterns

The excerpt given below is from lesson 6-A. Play the videotape and do the following activities.

1. Underline the words that receive the most stress and mark pauses with slashes (/).
2. Circle the words that are difficult to pronounce.
3. Read the paragraph yourself. Try it several times following the pauses and stress of the native speaker.

Lesson 6-A

Let's apply this graph to the example we did just a moment ago. When you carefully plot the function x to the sixth power, you find something that rises very steeply on both sides. Because it's an even power you get a positive number even when x is a negative number because it's multiplying by itself. The derivitive here, six x to the fifth—what is that derivative when x is zero? Class? [Zero.] Right. When you plug in zero for x, you get a derivative of zero. Here at x equals zero, here at the origin we verify that the tangent line is indeed horizontal, that is to say, it has a slope of zero, neither increasing which would be a positive slope, nor decreasing which would be a negative slope.

Fluency Work 2:
Explaining Graphs and Diagrams

Several different graphs and diagrams are shown below. Working in pairs, explain each graph or diagram to a partner. Focus on correct vocabulary in your explanations. If you are not sure what words to use for an explanation, write down vocabulary questions in the space provided.

When you finish the activity, ask your teacher or other students in the class your vocabulary questions. Write down the new words or phrases that you need.

1.

Air Pollutant Emissions by Pollutant and Source, 1970 to 1985
(In millions of metric tons, except lead in thousands of metric tons. Metric ton = 1.1023 short tons)

		Controllable Emissions							Percent of Total		
Year and Pollutant	Total Emissions	Transportation		Fuel Combustion[a]		Industrial Processes	Solid Waste Disposal	Misc. Uncontrollable	Transportation	Fuel Combustion	Industrial
		Total	Road Vehicles	Total	Electric Utilities						
1970:											
Carbon monoxide	98.7	71.8	62.7	4.4	.2	8.9	6.4	7.2	72.7	4.5	9.1
Sulfur oxides	28.2	.6	.3	21.3	15.8	6.2	—[b]	.1	2.1	75.5	22.0
Volatile organic compounds	27.2	12.4	11.1	1.1	—[b]	8.6	1.8	3.3	45.8	4.1	31.7
Particulates	18.1	1.2	.9	4.6	2.3	10.1	1.1	1.1	6.6	25.4	55.8
Nitrogen oxides	18.1	7.6	6.0	9.1	4.4	.7	.4	.3	42.0	50.3	3.9
Lead	203.8	163.6	156.0	9.6	.3	23.9	6.7	—[b]	80.3	4.7	11.7
1980:											
Carbon monoxide	76.0	52.6	45.3	7.3	.3	6.3	2.2	7.6	69.2	9.6	8.3
Sulfur oxides	23.2	.9	.4	18.7	15.5	3.5	—[b]	—[b]	3.9	80.6	15.1
Volatile organic compounds	22.8	8.2	6.9	2.2	—[b]	9.0	.6	2.9	36.0	9.6	39.5
Particulates	8.4	1.3	1.1	2.4	.8	3.2	.4	1.1	15.5	28.6	37.6
Nitrogen oxides	20.3	9.2	7.2	10.1	6.4	.7	.1	.2	45.3	49.8	3.4
Lead	70.6	59.4	56.4	3.9	.1	3.6	3.7	—[b]	84.1	5.5	5.1
1985:											
Carbon monoxide	67.5	47.5	40.7	8.1	.3	4.6	2.0	5.3	70.4	12.0	6.8
Sulfur oxides	20.7	.8	.5	17.0	14.2	2.9	—[b]	—[b]	3.9	82.1	14.0
Volatile organic compounds	21.3	7.2	6.0	2.6	—[b]	8.6	.6	2.3	33.8	12.2	40.4
Particulates	7.3	1.3	1.1	2.1	.6	2.7	.3	.8	17.8	28.8	37.0
Nitrogen oxides	20.0	8.9	7.1	10.2	6.8	.6	.1	.1	44.5	51.0	3.0
Lead	21.0	14.5	.9	.5	.1	2.3	2.8	—[b]	69.0	2.4	11.0

Source: U.S. Bureau of the Census, *Statistical Abstract of the United States: 1988* (Washington, D.C.: GPO, 1988), 192.
[a]Stationary.
[b]Less than 50,000 metric tons.

Vocabulary Questions

2.

Millions of Tons

[Line graph showing emissions from 1970 to 1980: Carbon Monoxide (around 100-105), Hydrocarbons, Sulfur oxides, Nitrogen oxides, and Particulates]

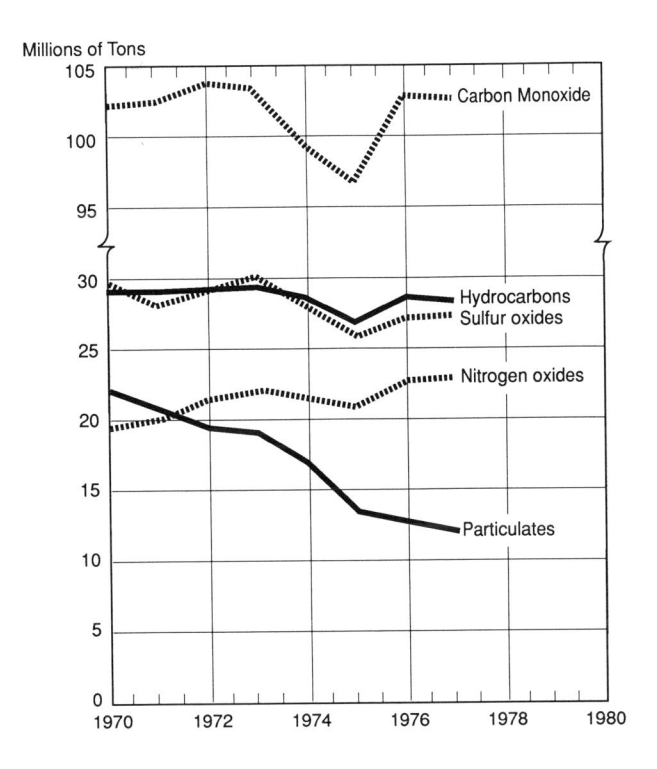

Vocabulary Questions

Source: U.S. Department of Commerce, Bureau of the Census, *Social Indicators III* (Washington, D.C.: GPO, 1980), 177.

3.

Hazardous Waste Sites–June 1987

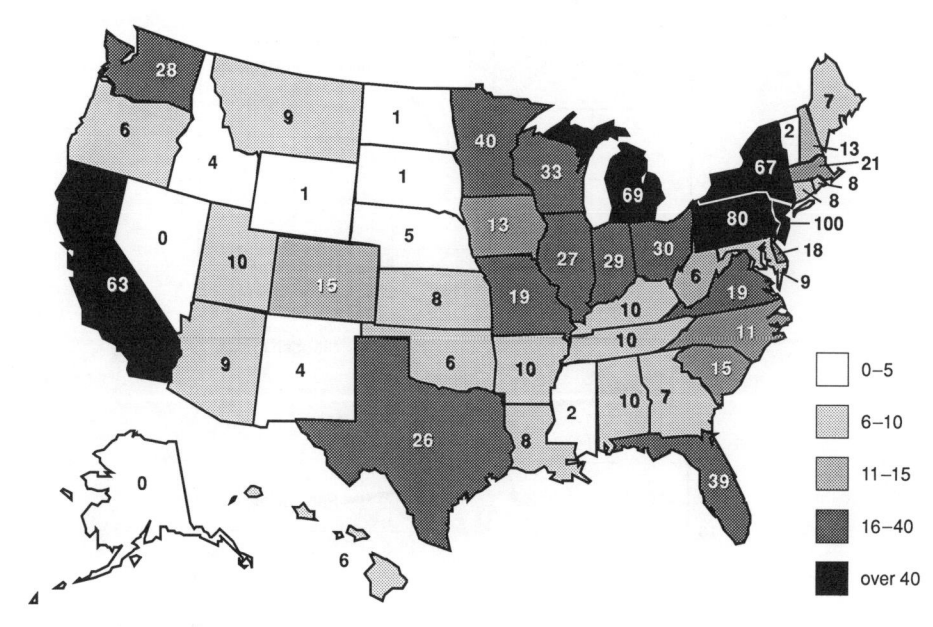

Total sites in U.S. 942[1]
Represents final and proposed sites on National Priority List.
[1] Includes eight in Puerto Rico and one in Guam.
Source: U.S. Environmental Protection Agency, National Priorities List Fact Book.

Vocabulary Questions

Source: U.S. Bureau of the Census, *Statistical Abstract of the United States: 1988* (Washington, D.C.: GPO, 1988) 193.

4.

Personal Consumption Expenditures for Recreation–
Percent Distribution: 1986

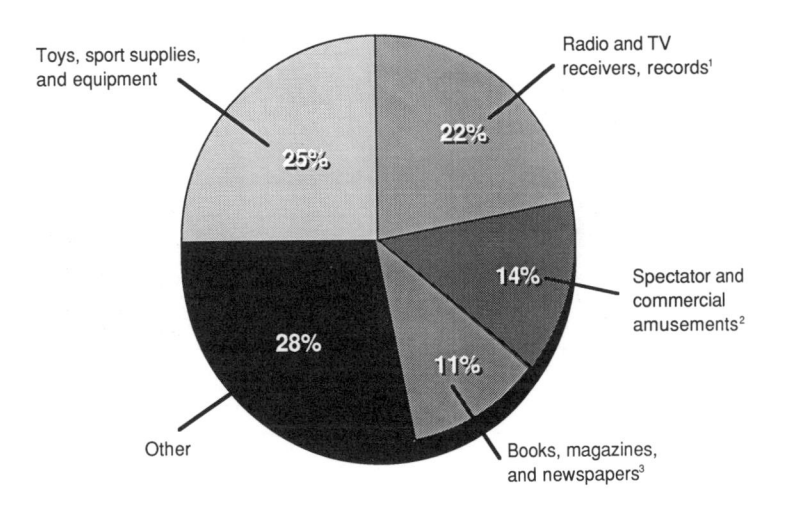

- Toys, sport supplies, and equipment — 25%
- Radio and TV receivers, records[1] — 22%
- Spectator and commercial amusements[2] — 14%
- Books, magazines, and newspapers[3] — 11%
- Other — 28%

[1] Includes musical instruments and radio and TV repair.
[2] Includes admissions to spectator amusements, commercial participant amusements, and pari-mutuel net receipts.
[3] Includes maps and sheet music.

Vocabulary Questions

Source: U.S. Bureau of the Census, *Statistical Abstract of the United States: 1988* (Washington, D.C.: GPO, 1988), 208.

5.   Corportate Profits: 1970 to 1986

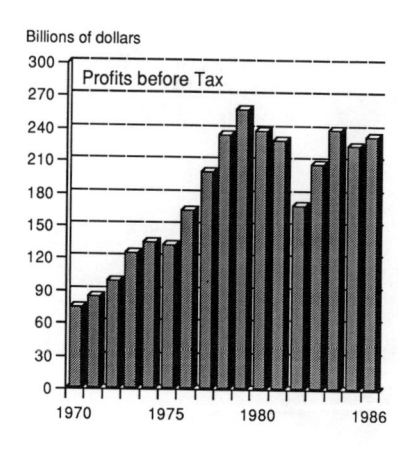

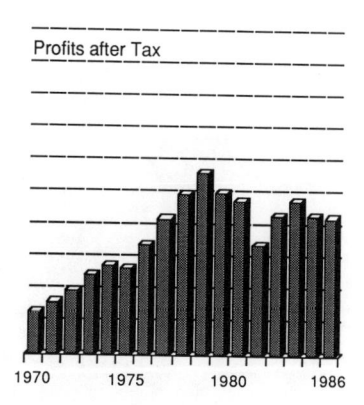

Vocabulary Questions

Source: U.S. Bureau of the Census, *Statistical Abstract of the United States: 1988* (Washington, D.C.: GPO, 1988), 492.

Graphs and Diagrams

Speech Patterns 1: The Language of Formulas

Many fields use mathematical formulas and there are conventional ways to read these formulas and the symbols they contain. Some of the more common formulas are listed here. Practice reading them out loud.

$f(x) = x$	f of x equals x
$f(x) = x^2$	f of x equals x squared
$f(x) = 3x^3 + 4$	f of x equals $3x$ cubed plus 4
	f of x equals $3x$ to the third plus 4
$f'(x) = 9x^2$	f prime of x equals $9x$ squared
$a(b+c)$	a times (b plus c)
x^n	x to the n
x^{n+1}	x to the n plus one
$1/x$	one over x
x_1	x one (or x sub one)
$\sqrt{2}$	the square root of 2
	root 2
$\lim_{x \to 0} 1/x^2$	the limit as x goes to zero of one over x squared
$x > 1$	x is greater than one
$x \geq 1$	x is greater than or equal to one
$x < 1$	x is less than one
$x \leq 1$	x is less than or equal to one
$f(x) = \sin x$	f of x equals sine x
$f(x) = \cos x$	f of x equals cosine x
$f(x) = \tan x$	f of x equals tangent x

Fluency Work 2: Saying Formulas

Choose some formulas common to your field and write them below. Read them out loud to a partner. Check with your teacher or someone in your field to make sure you are reading them correctly. If you are in a nonscience field, perhaps your field has some other information expressed in symbolic terms.

Formula 1:

Formula 2:

Formula 3:

Fluency Work 3: Speech Analysis

By speaking freely on tape and then analyzing your own speech, you can learn more about the patterns of your language. Follow these steps in analyzing your own speech.

1. Plan a short explanation of a graph. You may use one of the graphs in this unit or your own.

2. Tape-record your explanation of the graph in your own words; do not read a prepared speech. Spend 2 minutes or less.

3. Listen to the tape and carefully transcribe your exact words.

4. Make improvements in the grammar, vocabulary, wording, or content if you need to.

5. Mark your transcription to show which words are stressed and where the pauses belong. Underline the stressed words and mark pauses with slashes (/).

6. Circle any words that are difficult to pronounce. Practice these difficult words.

7. Read the passage from your transcription and tape-record it again. Compare the first version to the new version.

8. Put away your transcription. Explain the graph again in your own words and tape-record the explanation. Compare this version to the other versions.

Miniclass Assignment

Present a graph or diagram with information from your field to the class. Explain it clearly in simple language, following these suggestions.

1. Spend 5 to 7 minutes.

2. Use the board or a handout so that everyone can see your graph or diagram.

3. Use the Vocabulary Planner.

4. Video- or audiotape your miniclass.

Vocabulary Planner

List the specialized words and phrases you plan to use in your miniclass. Mark the stress patterns for each word or phrase. Circle any troublesome sounds. Practice pronouncing these important words and phrases before you teach your miniclass.

Word or Phrase   *Pronunciation Notes*

Self-Evaluation

If your miniclass was video- or audiotaped, watch or listen to the tape as you fill out this self-evaluation form.

1. What kind of graph or diagram did you use?

2. What did the students learn from your graph or diagram?

3. Is this graph commonly used in your field? Where did you get it?

4. What changes would you make if you had to do this miniclass again?

5. List any questions about grammar, pronunciation, or vocabulary.

Observation Assignment

You have now completed the first part of this book, on lectures. In this assignment, you will have a chance to see how teachers in your university organize their lectures.

Observe one or more lecture classes on your campus. Most instructors in large classrooms do not mind an extra observer as long as you ask permission first. If you are taking classes now, observe your own teachers. You may also wish to tape-record the lesson, with permission of the instructor, of course.

While you observe, make a lesson plan or outline of the lecture, similar to the example lesson plan given below. Pay attention to the different topics covered in units 1 through 6.

Activities

1. Compare your lesson plan with the lesson plans made by other students in the class. How are they similar or different? What makes the lessons effective or not effective?

2. Deliver the lecture (or part of the lecture) for the class or for a partner, using your own words. Follow the organization used by the instructor. You may wish to tape-record your lecture and then do a speech analysis.

3. If you tape-recorded the lecture, choose a small section of it and transcribe the lecturer's words. Analyze your transcription for stress patterns and pauses. Practice reading your transcript as a fluency exercise.

Sample Lesson Plan

This is an example of a lesson plan, taken from the Math class you have seen in the videotape "Techniques for Teachers."

Introduction

—review of last class

—outline of today's class, the derivative

Definition of derivative (includes lots of restatements)

—simple definition: "the rate of change"

—mathematical definition, formula on the board

—questions from students

Example: falling objects

—explanation of the problem

—calculations on the board

—questions from students

Example: children learning vocabulary
- —explanation of the problem
- —calculations on the board

Example: economics, marginal cost
- —explanation of the problem
- —calculations on the board

Conclusion
- —summary of the main points

Part II
Classroom Interaction

Unit 7

Student Questions 1

It is natural for students to ask questions, especially in a small class. In fact, those who ask questions are often very smart students who pay close attention and want to know more about the material. This unit deals with simple, straightforward questions, while unit 8 deals with difficult questions. There is one miniclass assignment for both units, at the end of unit 8.

These are some strategies for answering questions from students.

—When you pause for questions, be sure to wait long enough to give students a chance to think. Some students may be shy about raising their hands and need a little time to get up their courage.

—When a student asks a question, repeat the question. That way others in the class will hear it. Also, you can make sure that you understood the question correctly.

—You can encourage students who ask questions by making positive remarks such as "Good question" or "That's a good point."

—Use the board to help make your answer clear.

—If two students ask a question at the same time, one way to manage the interaction is to ask one of the students to wait, answer the other student's question, and then go back to the first student.

—After you have answered a question, look back to the student who asked the question to make sure he or she is satisfied with the answer.

Teachers in Action

(Play the videotape "Techniques for Teachers")

Lessons 7-A through 7-E show teachers answering questions from students. As you watch each lesson, write down the following information.

    a. What is the student's question?

    b. Does the teacher repeat the question? What words does he or she use to repeat the question.

    c. What encouragement does the teacher give, if any?

7-A. a. Question:

      b. Repeat?   What words?

      c. Encouragement:

7-B. a. Question:

      b. Repeat?   What words?

      c. Encouragement:

Student Questions 1

7-C. a. Question:

    b. Repeat?   What words?

    c. Encouragement:

    d. What phrase does the teacher use to acknowledge his error?

7-D. a. Question:

    b. Repeat?   What words?

    c. Encouragement:

7-E. a. Question:

    b. Repeat?   What words?

    c. Encouragement:

In lesson 7-F you see a situation in which two students ask a question at the same time. The teacher decides who will be first and asks the other to wait. Later she returns to the other student so that both students get a chance to speak.

While you watch, write down the words the teacher uses to manage the interaction. The first words for each sentence are given.

Lesson 7-F

Asking one student to wait:

Hold _____

Calling on the other student:

What _____

Returning to the first student:

Um, Jim _____

Language Models

These key sentences and phrases from the videotape are used for answering student questions. Study them carefully and add the ones you like to your own vocabulary.

    7-A   Before we move along to a more general interpretation of the derivative, are there any questions at this point?

            The question is, what is the role of h in the definition of the derivative.

            Let me put the formula back up and draw you a picture that'll show you what it's doing there.

    7-B   So I hope I've answered your question about the role of h in the definition.... Yes, Bill?

            The question is, does it matter how big h is?

    7-C   The question is, that doesn't seem reasonable because it appears to increase without limit.

            And let me just say that you're absolutely right, I should have said that the example applies in a vacuum only....

    7-F   Hold on just a sec, wait, what were you going to say?

            Jim, you had something that you were going to mention.

Speech Patterns 1: Questions in Class

Here is a trick to understand questions in class: Concentrate on the stress pattern of the sentence. The important content words in the sentence will have the strongest stress. Listen for the stressed words in the sentence and you will have a good clue to the content of the sentence.

For example, three ways to ask the same questions are listed below. Notice that the first one is very direct, but the second and third ones begin with polite phrases.

1. What is the *date* of the *quiz*?

2. I was wondering if you could tell us the *date* of the *quiz*?

3. *Excuse* me, did you happen to mention the *date* of the *quiz*?

Student Questions 1

Although each question is phrased differently, the same two words are stressed, *date* and *quiz*. If you only hear those two words, you can probably figure out the question. Usually the polite phrase at the beginning of a question is not stressed.

These are examples of questions that begin with a polite phrase. In each sentence, *underline* the words that receive the most stress. Compare your answers with a partner. Have your teacher or another native speaker of English read them for you.

1. Would you mind telling us how you graded this quiz?
2. Could you possibly explain that one more time?
3. Excuse me, but did you happen to mention the time of the exam?
4. Do you think you could give us an example of that?
5. Do you think you'd have time to review chapter 4?
6. So what you're saying is that there is no limit, right?
7. I'm sorry, you lost me there. Would you go through that again?
8. Yeah, I was just hoping that you would say something about the exam next week.
9. I'd be interested in knowing if that's true in other cases.
10. I just wanted to ask a question about the derivative.

Listening for Stressed Words

The words from the student's questions in lessons 7-A through 7-F are printed below with the stressed words missing. Play the tape again and identify the stressed words in the students' questions. Write them in the blanks. Do these words give you a clue to the main content of their questions?

7-A. I'm a little _____ about _____, it, what, what does it have to _____ with anything here. It seems to _____.

7-B. Does it _____ how _____ _____ is? It seems that if you go _____ _____, uh, to _____ and then work _____, um, it should give you the _____ _____ line. Is that _____?

7-C. Um, my _____ is about the _____ _____ that we talked about. Um, I've always heard that there's a _____ to how _____ things can

_____ but _____ seems to indicate that there _____ no limit, that, um, the _____ is always going to be _____ _____ something, um that it's a _____. Is that _____?

7-D. Functional features: do you mean _____ _____ to the _____?

7-E. If you think about _____, for example. You know these _____ tires are now popular on _____ bikes. Would you classify this as a _____ feature or a _____ feature in that case?

7-F. I, you _____, I was thinking, you _____ export _____ to _____. Guns are not _____, um, so I was just, I don't know what kind of _____ you'd call that, but....

Fluency Work 1: Using Native Speaker Patterns

The excerpt given below is from lesson 7-C. Play the videotape and do the following activities:

1. <u>Underline</u> the words that receive the most stress and mark pauses with slashes (/).
2. Circle the sounds that are difficult to pronounce.
3. Read the paragraph yourself. Try it several times until you feel a smooth fluency.

Lesson 7-C

The question is, my example here of the falling object which falls $16x$ squared feet after x seconds after being dropped and has a speed of 32 times x feet per second x seconds after being dropped. The question is, that doesn't seem reasonable because it appears to increase without limit. And let me just say, you're absolutely right, I should have said that this example applies in a vacuum only and that in real life, in the real world there is something called air resistance which acts against the pull of gravity and causes a falling object to reach what's called a terminal velocity which is its steady state at which the gravitational force pulling downward exactly balances the air resistance which is retarding it by pushing upward so this is only meant to apply for the first, say, few seconds and it would be more complicated after that.

Fluency Work 2: Repeating the Question

In this activity, practice calling on students and then repeating their questions. One person should go to the front of the room and the other students in the class should interview that person about his or her life by raising their hands and asking questions. The person at the front of the room calls on the students who raise their hands. Then, he or she must *repeat* the question before answering it, as shown in the following examples.

Question:	What is your major field?
Repeat and answer:	The question is, what is my major field. It's Chemistry.
Question:	Do you smoke?
Repeat and answer:	She is asking whether I smoke. Yes. I can't seem to quit!

This activity will also help you get to know other students in the class.

Comprehension Strategies

When you come to a foreign country for the first time, comprehension can be a problem, especially if the native speakers talk faster than you expect. Share your ideas about comprehension problems and how to solve them, using these suggestions to organize your ideas.

1. Think of a specific time when you had a comprehension problem with a native speaker of English.

2. Working in pairs, describe your situation to your partner and compare. Write down both of your experiences using the space below. You may add more if you like.

3. Compare your experiences with those of the rest of the class. Suggest ideas to solve each other's comprehension problems. Tell others what strategies have worked for you.

Situations that Cause Comprehension Problems

Strategies to Solve Comprehension Problems

Unit 8

Student Questions 2

Answering Difficult Questions

In this unit, we will discuss problems that can occur when students ask questions. Listed below are some of the most common problems classroom teachers face and some strategies that you can use to solve the problems.

An Inappropriate Question

If a question is inappropriate or does not fit into your plan, then you can politely tell the student that you do not have time to answer the question now. Perhaps the student can ask you the question again after class or during your office hours.

These are some polite phrases for this situation.

Would you mind asking me that during office hours?

I think I'd better stick to this material today.

Sorry, but I'd rather discuss that after class.

I'd rather not use class time for that.

A Question That Is Difficult to Understand

Sometimes it is hard to understand a student's question. This may be due to language problems or because the student does not make the meaning clear. In this case, you may ask the student to repeat his or her question or to ask it in a different way. You may also ask other students in the class if they can explain the question.

These are some phrases to handle questions that are hard to understand.

Sorry?

Pardon?

What?

Could you say that again?

I didn't understand what you said. Could you repeat it?

Could you say that again in a different way?

Another important strategy is to show a confused look on your face. By moving your eyebrows together, toward the center of your forehead, you will show that you don't understand. If a student sees a confused look, he or she is likely to repeat the question.

A Question Ahead of Its Time

If a student asks a question about something that you plan to explain in the future, you can say that you will answer the question later. These are some polite phrases for this situation.

Good question! We're going to cover that in the next class.

Why don't you save that question for the next unit.

I'll answer that question when we cover chapter 4.

A Question Already Covered

If a question arises about a topic that you have already explained, you may not feel like using class time to answer it. Politely tell the student where he or she can find the answer and move on. These are some polite phrases for this situation.

Maybe you weren't here, but we covered that last week.

If you'd like me to explain that again, come to my office.

You should have that in your notes from last week.

A Question That You Can't Answer!

If you do not know the answer to a question, you may simply tell the student that you do not know and you will find the information and bring the answer to the next class. You may also try asking other members of the class if they can answer the question. These are some polite phrases for this situation.

I'm afraid I don't know.

Good question! I don't know the answer.

Let me check that for you and I'll tell you next time.

Does anyone else know the answer to that question?

An Aggressive Question

There is no easy solution when a student challenges you or is rude to you in class. One suggestion is to speak to the person privately after class. Tell the person how his or her behavior affects the class. Explain your point of view in an honest way, and allow the student to explain his or hers.

Teachers in Action

(Play the videotape "Techniques for Teachers")

Lessons 8-A through 8-F show examples of students asking questions that cause some problems for the teachers. In each case, write down the reason the question causes a problem and describe how the teacher handles the situation.

8-A. What is the problem?

What does the teacher do?

8-B. What is the problem? (Is there a problem?)

What does the teacher do?

8-C. What is the problem?

What does the teacher do?

8-D. What is the problem?

What does the teacher do?

8-E. What is the problem?

What does the teacher do?

8-F. What is the problem?

What does the teacher do?

Language Models

These key sentences and phrases from lessons 8-A through 8-F may be useful for answering difficult questions in your own teaching situation.

8-A. My haircut? Actually my wife cut it, but let's get back to the material. Any questions about this graph please?

8-B. You can expect everything we've covered so far to be on the test.

8-C. Okay, well, let's finish up this material for right now and perhaps we can deal with this at the end of the hour or you can come by my office and we can go over it in office hours.

8-D. I'm sorry, I don't understand the question.... Hmm. I'm still not sure what you mean. Can you think of a different way of asking that?... I see. So you're asking, suppose you're given a derivative and you're asked to find the original function.... OK, that's advanced material. We'll be covering that in a few weeks.... But we'll do more on that in a few weeks.

8-E. I'm not quite sure I understand what you're asking. Perhaps you could point it out to me on the handout, what you're asking. . . . I'm sure you've got a good question here. Let's pursue it.

8-F. Some kind of extra point . . . um, can you elaborate? . . . That's a very good question. Ah, in that case the point is called an outlier and actually that's something I'd like to defer talking about until next lecture but we will get to it in the next lecture.

Fluency Work 1: Using Native Speaker Patterns

The excerpt given below is from lesson 8-E. Play the videotape and do the following activities.

1. <u>Underline</u> the words that receive the most stress and mark pauses with slashes (/).

2. Circle the words that are difficult to pronounce.

3. Read the passage out loud with a partner. Practice it several times to get a feel for the patterns of the speakers on the videotape. Switch partners and try it again.

Lesson 8-E

June: So, are there any questions? Yeah.

Elisabeth: Well, what if it's just a line?

June: If all the points fall exactly on a line the correlation coefficient will be either plus or minus one; is that what you mean?

Elisabeth: No, what if the graph is just a line?

June: I'm not quite sure I understand what you're asking. Perhaps you could point it out to me on the handout, what you mean.

Elisabeth: Ah, well, what . . . no, never mind.

June: No, no, let's, I think, I'm sure you've got a good question here, let's, let's pursue it.

Elisabeth: Well, what if it were just a line like this?

June: Oh, that's a very good question. Yes, what if, your question is, what if all the points fell on a horizontal line. Then the correlation coefficient will turn out to be zero in that case.

Fluency Work 2: Roleplay of a Miscommunication

Below are some situations in which a student and teacher misunderstand each other. Work with a partner and play out each situation for the rest of the class, following these suggestions.

1. Use any methods you can think of to resolve the confusion.
2. Use some of the polite phrases in the chapter.
3. Show your confusion on your face.
4. Have some fun with these situations—enjoy yourselves.

1. The teacher asks if there are any questions on a particular textbook. The student asks a question about another assignment given last week in another textbook.
2. The student asks if the final exam will be "open book." The teacher is not familiar with this term. The student continues to repeat the term "open book" several times. ("Open book" means that students may use textbooks and notes during the exam.)
3. The teacher is telling the students what textbooks to buy for class. The student asks the price of the books. The teacher does not know. The student asks what the hours of the bookstore are. The teacher does not know.
4. With a partner, make up a situation in which a student and teacher misunderstand each other.

Miniclass Assignment

Present a simple concept from your field to the class. Be prepared for students in the class to ask you questions. Beforehand, decide on three members of the class who will ask one question each. Of course others may ask too if they wish. Follow these suggestions.

1. Spend 5 to 7 minutes.
2. Use the strategies in this unit and in unit 7 in answering questions.
3. Use the Vocabulary Planner.
4. Video- or audiotape your miniclass.

Topic Idea: A Piece of Equipment

Bring an object used in your field and demonstrate its use to the class. Let students have a hands-on experience. The object doesn't need to be expensive or complex. Consider bringing a test tube, a calculator, a scale, a lens, a thermometer, or a map. If your object is large, you could bring a model or drawing of it. Surely people will have questions.

Vocabulary Planner

List the specialized words and phrases you plan to use in your miniclass. Mark the stress patterns for each word or phrase. Circle any troublesome sounds. Practice pronouncing these important words and phrases before you teach your miniclass.

Word or Phrase   *Pronunciation Notes*

Self-Evaluation

If your miniclass was video- or audiotaped, watch or listen to the tape as you fill out this self-evaluation form.

1. List all the questions that students asked you, then write down your answer.

    Question 1:

    Answer 1: (Did you repeat the question?)

    Question 2:

    Answer 2: (Did you repeat the question?)

    Question 3:

    Answer 3: (Did you repeat the question?)

    Use another page if there were more questions.

2. Do you think you answered the questions appropriately? Were the students satisfied with your answers? Why or why not?

3. Were there any communication problems? How were they resolved?

4. What changes would you make if you had to do this miniclass again?

5. List any questions about grammar, vocabulary, or pronunciation.

Unit 9

Brainstorming

Brainstorming is a technique used by some teachers to get all of their students involved in collecting a lot of information. The teacher asks a question and students in the class contribute ideas, either by raising their hands or by just speaking out. The teacher usually lists the ideas on the board. Brainstorming works best in a small class.

These are some suggestions for using brainstorming.

—Use this technique to get many people involved in the lesson. It is more interesting when everyone participates and students remember more if they give the ideas themselves.

—Allow enough time for people to think before they answer.

—Do not criticize people for their ideas. If people think they will be criticized, they will not speak up. Instead, use positive words to encourage students: "Yes," "good idea," "right," and "good suggestion."

—Try to accept even a "wrong" idea. Maybe you can change the idea a little bit to make it fit your class.

—You can contribute ideas, too, or give hints and suggestions to help the students.

—When a student gives an idea, repeat the idea so that others in the class can hear it. Also, if you repeat the idea you can make sure that you understood it clearly.

—If everyone is speaking at once and it seems too confusing, you may ask the students to raise their hands so that you can call on them one at a time.

At the end of the brainstorming activity, you have a long list of ideas. How can these ideas serve the purpose of your class? Now is the time to narrow down the list or make categories. Use the information to meet the goals of the class.

Teachers in Action

(Play the videotape "Techniques for Teachers")

Lessons 9-A through 9-C show a teacher using brainstorming activities. As you watch the lessons, write out the answers to these questions.

1. What is the main question that the students are trying to answer?

2. How does the brainstorming activity help the teacher meet the goals of the class?

9-A. 1. Main question(s):

2. How does it help meet the goals?

9-B. 1. Main question(s):

2. How does it help meet the goals?

9-C. Main question(s):

2. How does it help meet the goals?

Brainstorming　　　　　　　　　　　　　　　　　　　　93

Play the videotape again. This time listen for the words that the teacher uses when she hears the students' ideas. Sometimes she repeats the student's words; sometimes she gives encouragement. List as many words and phrases as you can.

9-A.

9-B.

9-C.

Why Use Brainstorming?

Notice that this teacher could have presented all this information in lecture form. However, there are several advantages to using a brainstorming activity.

—It is lively and interesting; no one is bored.

—Students may remember the ideas better when they think of them themselves.

—The teacher can be sure that the students understand the points because they are saying them out loud.

—Students will try to be prepared for class if they know they will be called on to speak.

Can you think of any other advantages of brainstorming?

Can you think of any disadvantages of brainstorming?

Language Models

The excerpts given below are from Lessons 9-A through 9-C, the brainstorming activities. Add the ones you like to your own vocabulary.

> 9-A. The most important question to ask is, what need does it satisfy?... So what else? What other things can you think of?... And how would that differ from the same company taking a bicycle to China?... What need does a bicycle satisfy in China?
>
> 9-B. Now, what other things do you think you have to consider?... What types of things do those government regulations affect?
>
> 9-C. What are some things that you can think of that you might be trying to export from Washington state?

Fluency Work 1: Using Native Speaker Patterns

The excerpt given below is from lesson 9-A. Play the videotape and do the following activities.

1. <u>Underline</u> the words that have the most stress and mark pauses with slashes (/).
2. Circle the words that are difficult to pronounce.
3. Join some other students and read the text out loud to get a feel for the quick interaction.

Lesson 9-A

Daphne: So, if you are a French company bringing a bicycle into the United States, what need would that bicycle satisfy? What does the customer need a bicycle for in the United States?

Kate: Transportation?

Daphne: Transportation.

Barbara: Recreation?

Becky: Leisure.

Daphne: Leisure.

Jim: Fashion.

Daphne: Fashion?

Jim: Well...

Daphne: Maybe.

Jim: You'd want to get a French bicycle cause it's from France. You know, we have this thing in our head that says that...

Daphne: OK, so status. It might have a certain amount of status involved with it. OK. And how would that differ from the same French company taking the bicycle to China? What's, what need does a bicycle satisfy in China?

Becky: Everyday transportation.

Daphne: Uh huh. OK, so you see a clear difference in terms of the basic function of a bicycle in those two different markets.

Fluency Work 2: Brainstorming

Go to the front of the class and lead a brainstorming session on one of the following questions. Organize the ideas on the board. Try to find some logical categories in which to group the answers. Repeat the answers you hear and use positive words to encourage response.

After you finish brainstorming, discuss how the class could use this information to meet the goals of a lesson.

1. What do you think of when you hear the word *Korea*? (Substitute any country you wish.)

2. Let's make a list of possible ways to solve the problem of crime in U.S. society.

3. What are some common problems that foreign students have in the United States?

4. (Choose one of the problems raised in question 3) Let's see if we can come up with some solutions to this problem.

5. Give me some examples of what modern governments do for society. What do we get for our taxes? (Maybe expand this to different countries.)

6. What are some of the sources of pollution in modern society?

7. Who can tell me some of the properties of air (water, a triangle, etc.)

8. Make suggestions about how to save money in modern society.

Miniclass Assignment

Lead a brainstorming activity with a topic from your field. Make it simple so everyone can understand. This is a good way to get people from other fields interested in yours. Follow these suggestions in planning your miniclass.

1. Spend 5 to 7 minutes.

2. Repeat the ideas that you hear and write them on the board.

3. Use positive words such as "right," and "good idea," to encourage students.

4. Draw a conclusion at the end of the brainstorming activity so that it meets your teaching goal.

5. Use the Vocabulary Planner.

6. Video- or audiotape your miniclass.

Vocabulary Planner

List the specialized words and phrases you plan to use in your miniclass. Mark the stress patterns for each word or phrase. Circle any troublesome sounds. Practice pronouncing these important words and phrases before you teach your miniclass.

Word or Phrase   *Pronunciation Notes*

Word or Phrase   *Pronunciation Notes*

Self-Evaluation

If your miniclass was video- or audiotaped, watch or listen to the tape as you fill out this self-evaluation form.

1. What was the main question(s) that you asked?

2. Describe what happened in your brainstorming activity. What did you say? What did others say? Did you use the board?

3. Was there any point where you lost control of the activity? If yes, what did you do?

4. How did you conclude the activity?

5. What did your brainstorming activity teach the class members?

Unit 10

Problem Solving

A good way to get the students involved in a class is to have them solve problems and answer questions during the class. Asking a question gives students a chance to think through the material of the lesson themselves and setting up problems for students to solve helps them apply their theoretical knowledge to practical situations.

These are some suggestions for using questions and problems in class.

—If you are reviewing material from other lessons, ask the students to tell you the main points.

—If you are presenting new information, you can challenge and interest the students by asking them to guess what some of your main points will be before you say them.

—If you are doing calculations on the board, ask the students if they can calculate the answers for you.

—Use questions and problems to review the homework. Instead of telling the students the answers, ask them to tell you.

—If a student raises a question in class, you may be able to help that student answer his or her own question by asking another question right back.

Teachers in Action

(Play the videotape "Techniques for Teachers")

Lessons 10-A through 10-E show teachers asking questions and posing problems to students in class. For each lesson, write down the questions that the teacher asks and note whether or not the teacher restates the students' answers.

10-A. Question 1:

Question 2:

Restatement of the answers?

10-B. Question 1:

Question 2:

Restatement of the answers?

10-C. Question 1:

Question 2:

Restatement of the answers?

10-D. Question 1:

Question 2:

Question 3:

Question 4:

Restatement of the answers?

10-E. Question:

Restatement of the answers?

Encouraging Students to Talk in Class

In lessons 10-A through 10-E, all the teachers get the answers they want to their questions. But what if you ask a question and no one answers? These are some suggestions for encouraging students to answer questions in class.

- —After a question, wait long enough to give students a chance to think.
- —Walk forward toward the students and ask the question again. Your body language will show the students that you really want them to try to answer your question.
- —Try asking your question in a different, or perhaps simpler way.
- —Call on a specific person by name: "Kim, do you know?"
- —When students do respond, try to give positive feedback: "Right" or "Good."
- —Try not to criticize students, even if they are wrong. The more open you are to everyone's ideas, the safer students will feel to participate.
- —When you ask a question and you receive an answer, restate the answer so that the others in the class can hear it.

Speech Patterns 1: Question Intonation

Remember these simple rules for question intonation.

1. Wh- questions are questions that begin with what, where, when, who, which, why, how.

   A Wh- question usually has a *falling* pitch pattern. This is the same intonation as a statement.

   Statement: You see a line in this plot.

   Question: What do you see in this plot?

2. Yes/No questions are questions that can be answered with a "yes" or a "no."

    A Yes/No question usually has a *rising* pitch pattern.

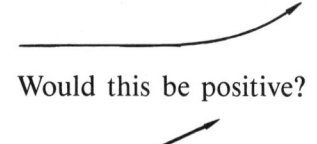

    Would this be positive?

    Any questions? (This is a short form of the Yes/No question "Are there any questions?")

3. A statement can be used as a question.
    Use a *rising* pitch and leave a piece of information missing at the end.

    Lesson 10-D: This one's got _____? (positive correlation)

4. Questions have sentence stress (see unit 1 for the rules of sentence stress).

    In a Wh- question, the sentence stress is just like a statement.

    Statement: This is the *strongest* correlation.

    Question: Which is the *strongest* correlation?

    In a Yes/No Question, pitch rises on the most important word of the sentence, and then continues to go up from there.

    Is it a *positive* number that we see?

5. In a question with *or*, the listener is supposed to choose between two contrasting ideas. Be sure to stress the two contrasting ideas strongly.
    The first idea should have a *rising* pitch and the second idea should have a *falling* pitch.

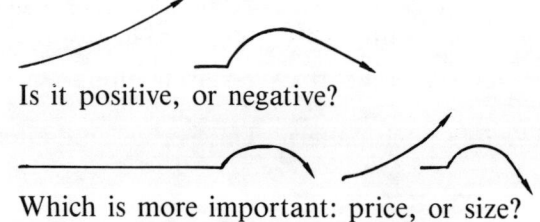

    Is it positive, or negative?

    Which is more important: price, or size?

Fluency Work 1: Using Native Speaker Patterns

Keeping the rules about question intonation in mind, mark these sentences from lessons 10-A through 10-E as follows. Then read them out loud, following your marks. Play the videotape again, if you need to.

a. Draw arrows above the sentence to show falling or rising pitch ↗ ↘

b. <u>Underline</u> the words that receive the most stress and mark pauses with slashes (/).

c. Circle the sounds or words that are difficult to pronounce.

10-A. What would the derivative of x^6 be, class?

10-A. How did you get that?

10-B. The derivative here, $6x^5$, what is that derivative when x is zero, class?

10-B. What happens when x is negative?

10-B. When you raise a negative number to the fifth power, is it positive or negative?

10-C. What do you see in this plot?

10-C. How would you describe the basic shape of this plot?

10-D. This one's got—what kind of correlation?

10-E. How would you find out about disposable income?

10-E. Where would you go to find that information?

Fluency Work 2: Forming Questions and Problems*

Listed below are some simple statements of fact. For each statement, form a question or problem. Work with a partner. This activity is more useful if the listener covers the page and tries to understand your speaking. Do not forget question intonation.

---

*Adapted with permission from J. Swales and P. Rounds, *College Classroom Discourse* (Ann Arbor: The English Language Institute, University of Michigan, 1985).

Statement: If $f(x) = 3x$ and $x = 0$, then $f(x) = 0$.

Question: If $f(x) = 3x$ and $x = 0$, then what does $f(x)$ equal?

1. If $f(x) = 4x + 1$, and $x = 4$, then $f(x) = 17$.
2. If $f(x) = 3x$, and $x < 0$, then $f(x)$ is negative.
3. A triangle has three angles.
4. The three angles of a triangle add up to 180 degrees.
5. If two angles of a triangle add up to 120 degrees, then the third angle is 60 degrees.
6. If the Japanese Yen rises against the U.S. dollar, Japanese products become more expensive in the United States.
7. If the supply of goods remains constant and demand increases, prices will increase.
8. The mean of 4, 5, 1, 10, and 15 is 7.
9. The median of 4, 5, 1, 10, and 15 is 5.
10. The reason the answers to questions 8 and 9 are different is that the mean is the average while the median is the middle number.

Write three simple facts from your field. Form a question so that students in the class will discover the fact.

1. Fact:

    Question:

2. Fact:

    Question:

3. Fact:

    Question:

Miniclass Assignment

Present a simple concept from your field to the class. Include questions and problems in your miniclass, following these suggestions.

1. Spend 5 to 7 minutes.
2. Use as many questions and problems as you can.
3. Use the Vocabulary Planner.

4. When people answer your questions, repeat their answers so others in the class can hear.

5. Do not criticize people for wrong answers.

6. Video- or audiotape your miniclass.

Topic Idea: Understanding Data

Bring a quantitative data set from your field to the class. If you do not normally work with quantitative data yourself, go to the library and find a data set in a professional journal from your field. Put the data set on a handout for the class. To make sure that everyone understands your data set, ask some questions about the content of your handout. Then ask people to do some simple calculations of averages or percentages from your data set.

Vocabulary Planner

List the specialized words and phrases you plan to use in your miniclass. Mark the stress patterns for each word or phrase. Circle any troublesome sounds. Practice pronouncing these important words and phrases before you teach your miniclass.

Word or Phrase   *Pronunciation Notes*

Self-Evaluation

If your miniclass was video- or audiotaped, watch or listen to the tape as you fill out this self-evaluation form.

1. What questions or problems did you pose? (List more on a separate page if necessary.)

    a.

    b.

    c.

    d.

2. For each question above, mark the correct intonation pattern by drawing a line above the question.

3. Describe what happened when you asked these questions. Were people able to answer your questions? If not, why not?

4. Did the students learn from these activities? How can you tell?

5. What changes would you make if you were teaching this class again?

6. List any questions about grammar, vocabulary, or pronunciation.

Unit 11

Discussion

Classroom discussion is an important part of the learning experience in North American colleges and universities. You may wish to encourage students to discuss their opinions or interpretations of course materials. By expressing their ideas in discussion, students develop a better understanding of the course material, and of their own and others' points of view. Class discussions also prepare students to articulate their ideas in written papers or tests. How is discussion used in your field?

The Discussion Leader

As a teacher, you are probably the leader of most classroom discussions. You can have a strong effect on how the discussion goes. These are some suggestions for leading a successful discussion.

—Encourage an open and supportive class atmosphere. Students will be more likely to talk in class if they feel their opinions will be taken seriously. If you ridicule or criticize students' ideas, or allow others to do so, students are likely to stop talking.

—Provide clear and interesting discussion questions. If your discussion questions are clearly focused, students will have an easier time responding to them.

—See that everyone has a chance to participate. If certain students do all the talking, you, as the teacher, are in a position to give others a chance.

—Keep the discussion moving. Draw conclusions from what people say and have more questions ready. Keep track of the time. If someone is talking too long, or on an unrelated topic, you may politely remind them to stick to the point.

Discussion Participation

There are many ways to participate in a discussion. Listed below are common ways to participate, followed by explanations and examples of each.

—Asking for information

—Giving information

—Asking for opinions

—Giving opinions

—Clarifying

—Managing

—Drawing Conclusions

Asking for Information

Asking for information usually means asking for facts. Participants in a discussion often ask each other for information about the topic. The teacher can encourage discussion by asking students for information. If a student gives a personal opinion, others may ask him or her for information that supports that opinion. These are examples of asking for information.

Does anyone know who won the election?

Has anyone heard what happened in the election?

Can you tell us about the results of the election, Clara?

Who can tell us about the outcome of the election?

Do you have any evidence that the election was unfair?

Giving Information

People give information in dicussions for several reasons. First, everyone in the discussion needs to understand the facts. Information is also given to support opinions. Often, reporting words, such as *I've read* or *I've heard,* are used to give information. Such words help prove that the information being given is true.

> I've heard that only 50 percent of the people voted in the election.
>
> I read in the paper that only 50 percent of the people voted in the election.
>
> Everyone is saying that only 50 percent of the people voted in the election.
>
> The fact is that only 50 percent of the people voted in the election.

Asking for Opinions

An opinion is a feeling, belief, or point of view. Participants in a discussion may ask for the opinions of others in the group. The teacher may also encourage members of the group to voice their opinions.

> What is your opinion about the results of the election?
>
> What do you think about the election?
>
> Do you think the election was fair or rigged?
>
> Let's get some other opinions about the election.

Giving Opinions

Participants in a discussion often give their opinions or points of view. Not everyone always agrees; there may be several different opinions about an issue.

> I think that the election was rigged.
>
> Oh really? In my opinion, the election was fair!
>
> I agree with Clara that the election was rigged.
>
> I disagree with Bonnie that the election was fair.
>
> I was disappointed in the outcome of the election.
>
> You were? Personally, I thought it was a historic event.

After giving an opinion, you can support your opinion with information. This will make your point stronger.

> My opinion is that the election was fair because several international agencies were watching the polls.

I myself believe that the election was a joke. I read that only 50 percent of the people voted.

Clarifying

Clarifying means making something clear. Ask for clarification if you cannot understand someone's point, or if the point is confusing. If others misunderstand your point, make it clear by rephrasing it or explaining it again.

> Are you saying that the election was rigged?
>
> No, I'm saying that it was poorly attended.
>
> I don't understand what you mean.
>
> I mean that the election was unfair.
>
> What do you mean by unfair?
>
> Could you say that again? I didn't get it.

Managing

Managing refers to participation that guides the discussion. Getting everyone involved, moving the discussion along, keeping track of the time, and reminding people to stick to the point are all forms of managing. In a classroom discussion, the teacher usually does most of the managing.

> Does anyone else have an opinion on this?
>
> Let's hear from some others. Clara?
>
> Clara, do you agree with Bonnie?
>
> Just a minute, Bonnie. What's your opinion, Clara?
>
> Let's move on to the next question.
>
> I'm afraid we're running out of time.
>
> We have time for one more comment.
>
> Could we agree to disagree for now?
>
> Let's get back to the main question.

Drawing Conclusions

In order to keep the discussion in focus, you, as the leader, may draw conclusions from what people say. Make a summary of ideas or show a connection among ideas. Explain how the points made in the discussion relate to the course material. This helps move the discussion along. It also helps people understand how one idea is related to another.

Bonnie, what you just said supports what Clara was saying before.

Most of us seem to agree that the election was rigged.

So, we can conclude that there were some problems with the election. Let me write them on the board.

This is very similar to what we discussed last week.

Can you relate what you just said to the reading?

Teachers in Action

(Play the videotape "Techniques for Teachers")

Lesson 11-A shows a short section of a discussion among the students in a marketing seminar. Play the videotape one or more times to understand the content.

Now, play the videotape again. This time follow the excerpt below as you listen. Notice the different types of participation are written in brackets, such as [Giving Opinions], [Managing], etc.

Some of the brackets are left empty, like this [_____]. Try to fill in the missing labels for these empty brackets (the answers are printed at the end of this unit).

Daphne: [Managing] Um, Jim, you had something that you were gonna mention.

Jim: [1._____] I, you can't, I was thinking, you can't export guns to Japan.

Becky: I was thinking of that too.

Jim: [2._____] Guns are not legal, um, so I was just, I don't know what kind of category you'd call that but...

Daphne: [Drawing Conclusions] OK, so legal...

Jim: [Clarifying] Legality, yeah.

Daphne: [Drawing Conclusions] ...illegal goods.

[3._____] Or alcohol to Saudi Arabia.

Jim: Right. Right.

Becky: [Giving Information] I can't remember exactly what the products were but um, we tried to export some things to Japan, things that we use every day and they bombed in Japan.

[4._____] Can you remember what any of those are?

[5._____] Like things we use every day here in the Western World...

Jim: No, I was just wondering...

Becky: [Clarifying]...was a big thing in Japan so we, so some of the companies tried to export it and it just bombed flat. I can't think of it.

[Giving Information] Maybe hamburger makers or, I'm not sure what, what the products were.

[6._____] but in a sense, you need to consider the culture and the daily activities, like is this product gonna even find its place, you know?

Jim: Yeah.

Barbara: [Giving Opinion] That's true, but that advertising is also a strong factor there.

Barbara: [7._____] I've heard somewhere, for example, if you're in Japan, they won't let you advertise your cars, American cars, in Japanese; they have to be advertised in English. So you're not, you know, the Japanese aren't going to get the information about the product that, that, you know, they would if it were in their own language,

[8._____] I mean, so what? Is that 'cause the product bombs? Or is that the result of being, um, having restricted advertising regulations?

Daphne: [9._____] Right, so they interrelate, a lot of these things.

Fluency Work 1: Using Native Speaker Patterns

The previous section contains the dialogue for lesson 11-A. Play the videotape again and do the following activities.

1. Underline the words that have the most stress and mark pauses with slashes (/).
2. Use arrows ╱ ╲ to show rising and falling intonation.
3. Circle the words that are difficult to pronounce.
4. Join some other students and read the text out loud to get a feel for the quick interaction. If you are working alone, practice some of the lines that you like best.

Fluency Work 2: Opinions versus Information

Several discussion topics are listed below. Working in pairs, ask your partner for some information about each topic and then ask for some opinions about the topic. Partners should answer the questions with information or opinions as appropriate. You may use phrases from this unit.

Topic: Your living situation

    a. Asking for information: Where do you live?

    b. Giving information: In university housing.

    c. Asking for opinion: What do you think of your living situation?

    d. Giving opinion: I think it's a very nice place, but it's too noisy for me.

1. Topic: Your classes
2. Topic: Your department
3. Topic: Your campus
4. Topic: The local climate
5. Topic: The local restaurants
6. Topic: Salaries at universities

7. Topic: Any recent event in the news
8. Topic: The economic situation in any country
9. Topic: Marriage and dating customs
10. Topic: Television

Fluency Work 3: Speech Analysis

By speaking freely on tape and then analyzing your own speech, you can learn more about the patterns of your language. Follow these steps in analyzing your own speech.

1. Choose a recent event in the news and think about it. Decide what your opinion is about the event.
2. Tape-record your explanation of the event and your opinion about it.
3. Listen to the tape and carefully transcribe your exact words.
4. Make improvements in the grammar, vocabulary, wording, or content if you need to.
5. Mark your transcription to show which words are stressed and where the pauses belong. Underline the stressed words and mark pauses with slashes (/).
6. Circle any words that are difficult to pronounce. Practice these difficult words.
7. Read the passage from your transcription and tape-record it again. Compare the first version to the new version.
8. Put away your transcription. Explain the event again in your own words and tape-record your explanation. Compare this version to the other versions.

Miniclass Assignment

Choose a discussion topic and lead a classroom discussion on that topic. Review the different types of participation mentioned in this unit. You are the leader, so pay particular attention to asking for information, asking for opinions, managing, and drawing conclusions. Follow these suggestions in planning the discussion.

1. Choose a topic that everyone will know something about.
2. Prepare some questions that ask for information and opinions.
3. Have someone in the class fill out the Discussion Checklist for your discussion (see page 116).

Discussion

4. Use the Question Planner.

5. Video- or audiotape your discussion.

Suggested Topic: A Recent Event in the News

Question Planner

It is important to prepare discussion questions that are easy to understand. Write down your questions in the space below. Which questions are asking for information? Which questions are asking for opinions? Make sure you can pronounce the words in your questions clearly.

Question   *Pronunciation Notes*

Discussion Checklist

Most of the members of the class will participate in the discussions. However, one or two people should stay outside the discussions and fill out the Discussion Checklist.

Fill in the class members' names below the numbers at the top of the chart. Put a small mark in the appropriate box when each person speaks. Do the best you can, it is not easy to catch everything.

After each discussion is over, look at the checklist carefully. What do you notice? Were certain people dominating the discussion? Were certain people silent? What roles did the leader play? Were conclusions drawn? Discuss this discussion.

	Leader	Students' Names				
Participation Role		#1	#2	#3	#4	#5
Asking for information						
Giving information						
Asking for opinions						
Giving opinions						
Clarifying						
Managing						
Drawing conclusions						
Other						

Self-Evaluation

If your discussion was video- or audiotaped, watch or listen to the tape as you fill out this evaluation form.

1. What was the topic of your discussion?

2. Describe the discussion. What happened?

3. Did anything unexpected happen in your discussion? Explain.

4. What changes would you make if you had to do this again?

5. List any questions about grammar, vocabulary, or pronunciation.

Observation Assignment

Observe how discussion is used in your field. In classes? In department meetings? In seminars?

Pay attention to a particular discussion in your department, perhaps at a department meeting. Who was the leader? Which types of participation did you notice?

Watch a television talk show that presents discussions of recent social and political events and identify the types of participation. Use the Participation Checklist if you wish.

Answers to Types of Participation in the Discussion (from page 111)

1. Giving information
2. Giving information
3. Giving information
4. Asking for information
5. Clarifying
6. Giving opinion
7. Giving information
8. Asking for opinion
9. Drawing conclusion

Unit 12

Putting Students to Work

Classroom Management

In some classes it is appropriate for the students to work on problems, projects, or experiments in the classroom. For example, solving problems in pairs or in small groups helps students understand the course material better because they can share their knowledge. Similarly, students can work together to answer focus questions about a reading.

Lab experiments are another obvious example of students working in class. Doing lab experiments is essential in most science fields. Lab work teaches students how to apply their theoretical knowledge to real experiments. Demonstrating how lab equipment works is also an important classroom activity. Know the safety features of your lab and show students how to use the equipment safely and correctly.

Activities such as these have both a learning and a testing purpose: the students gain a greater understanding of the course material, and the teacher can assess that understanding. Many of these classroom activities require the teacher to provide management and direction. Simple directions, given with confidence, help students carry out the activities most effectively.

Teachers in Action

(Play the videotape "Techniques for Teachers")

Lessons 12-A and 12-B show two different classroom activities. For each lesson, answer these questions.

    12-A. Describe the activity:

        What is the learning purpose?

        What is the testing purpose?

        The teacher has a problem when he asks for volunteers. What is the problem? How does he solve it?

        Would you ever use an activity like this? Why or why not?

    12-B. Describe the activity:

        What is the learning purpose?

        What is the testing purpose?

        Would you ever use an activity like this? Why or why not?

Language Models

The excerpts given below are from lessons 12-A and 12-B in which teachers give directions to their students. Study the excerpts carefully; you may wish to add some of these phrases to your own vocabulary.

Putting Students to Work 121

Lesson 12-A.   Now, I'd like some volunteers of people to do the homework problems at the board.

    Volunteers please?

    Why don't you do number one at this part of the board.

    Please do number two here in the middle.

    I would be careful to write that beginning here is the derivative...

    Please raise your hand if you agree. Please raise your hand if you disagree.

    Again just to tidy up the notation here, write an equals sign in between so it doesn't look like those symbols are running into each other.

Lesson 12-B.   I'd like you to form yourselves into pairs.

    Each pair should take a white sheet and a yellow sheet.

    Use the yellow sheet to draw your graph on.

    Then go ahead and answer the questions that are on the handout. So form yourselves into pairs.

    You might as well work with the person sitting next to you.

    Let's discuss some of the answers now.

    I think we'll just go around the room and the different groups can give me answers to the questions.

Fluency Work 1: Using Native Speaker Patterns

The excerpt given below is from lesson 12-B. Play the videotape and do the following activities.

1. <u>Underline</u> the words that have the most stress and mark pauses with slashes (/).
2. Circle the words that are difficult to pronounce.
3. Read the text out loud. Try it several times until you feel a smooth fluency.

Lesson 12-B

Now I have some work that I'd like you to do here in class. I'd like you to form yourselves into pairs or if there's an odd person, you can have a triple. Here's the assignment. It's a set of data about how broad trees are at their bases and we'll look at how well it's correlated with how large the tree is in terms of volume. Each pair should take a white sheet and a yellow sheet. Use the yellow sheet to draw your graph on, and then go ahead and answer the questions that are on the handout. So form yourselves into pairs; you might as well work with the person sitting next to you.

Fluency Work 2: Giving Directions

Listed below are some common classroom activities. They are simple activities, but they require classroom management and clear directions. Give directions for each activity to the class in your own words, using some of the phrases from the Language Models section of this unit. Be firm and make your directions simple and clear.

1. Pass a piece of paper around the class and have the class members list their names and fields on the paper.

2. Ask the people in the class to line up in alphabetical order by last name.

3. Ask each person to briefly introduce himself or herself to the class.

4. Ask people in the room to line up in order of the length of time spent in this country.

5. Choose five people to go to the blackboard. Ask each person to write his or her name and address on their blackboard space.

6. Ask the class to work together to make a calendar that shows the important dates of this quarter or semester at your university.

7. Put the class members into groups of two. Ask each pair to write down three suggestions for new international students coming to this country. Afterwards, ask each group to report their suggestions to the rest of the class.

8. Pretend you are scheduling individual conferences with each student in the class. Make a schedule on paper so that every class member gets an appointment with you.

Fluency Work 3: Speech Analysis

By speaking freely on tape and then analyzing your own speech, you can learn more about the patterns of your language. Follow these steps in analyzing your own speech.

1. Choose one of the classroom activities listed above or an activity that might be used in your field. Before you begin, think about the steps involved in giving directions for the activity.

2. Briefly tape-record your directions for the activity; do not read a prepared speech.

3. Listen to the tape and carefully transcribe your exact words.

4. Make improvements in the grammar, vocabulary, wording, or content if you need to.

5. Mark your transcription to show which words are stressed and where the pauses belong. <u>Underline</u> the stressed words and mark pauses with slashes (/).

6. Circle any words that are difficult to pronounce. Practice these difficult words.

7. Read the passage from your transcription and tape-record it again. Compare the first version to the new version.

8. Put away your transcription. Give the directions again in your own words and tape-record them. Compare this version to the other versions.

Miniclass Assignment

Organize a classroom activity in which the class members have to solve a problem, do an experiment, or otherwise involve themselves in some kind of work. Explain the activity before they start the work, making sure your directions are clear. Be prepared to help people if necessary, and follow these suggestions.

1. Bring any equipment, handouts, etc., as needed.

2. Break the activity down into simple steps.

3. Be prepared for questions.

4. Use the Vocabulary Planner.

5. Video- or audiotape your miniclass.

Vocabulary Planner

List the specialized words and phrases you plan to use in your miniclass. Mark the stress patterns for each word or phrase. Circle any troublesome sounds. Practice pronouncing these words and phrases before you teach your miniclass.

Word or Phrase   *Pronunciation Notes*

Self-Evaluation

If your miniclass was video- or audiotaped, watch or listen to the tape as you fill out this evaluation form.

1. What activity did you have the students do? What was the learning purpose? What was the testing purpose?

2. Describe what happened.

3. What did the students learn?

4. What changes would you make if you had to do this again?

5. List any questions about grammar, vocabulary, or pronunciation.

Part III
Office Hours

Unit 13

One on One: Interacting with Individuals

In North American colleges and universities, most teachers hold office hours for students to ask questions and discuss problems individually. This type of one-to-one interaction involves some different communication strategies than teaching in a classroom. In this unit we will discuss six of these strategies.

—Listening actively

—Checking understanding

—Using pencil and paper

—Understanding and using body language

—Giving encouragement

—Saying "no" politely

Listening Actively

In an office hour, communication moves in two directions. Listening is as important as speaking. By actively listening to the student, a teacher can show interest in the student's problem and better understand what the student is talking about.

These are some suggestions for active listening.

1. Look at the speaker's eyes while he or she is speaking. This shows that you are listening carefully.

2. When the speaker pauses, say "uh huh" or "mm hmm" with rising intonation to show that you are ready for him or her to continue.

3. When the speaker stops talking, summarize what you think he or she has said to be sure that you understand.

4. Clarify any points of misunderstanding as soon as they occur.

Checking Understanding

While Listening

It is possible that you, the teacher, do not understand what the student is saying. Be sure to stop the student as soon as you do not understand, before the misunderstanding gets worse. These simple phrases can be used to express your possible misunderstanding of a student's question or problem.

"What?"

"Sorry?"

"Pardon?"

"Excuse me?"

"Wait a minute. What did you say?"

"Could you say that again?"

"Could you slow down a bit?"

"Would you say that again in a different way?"

Another way to check your understanding is to summarize what you think the student has said. If you are wrong, the student can say what he or she said before in a different way.

"So, you're saying that you want me to excuse you from class?" "Are you asking me to explain the third problem?"

Finally, by simply showing a confused look on your face, you can signal the student to stop and repeat.

If you check understanding at every step, you can help the communication go more smoothly.

While Speaking

Picture this common situation.

> A student comes to a teacher's office to get some extra help with the course material. The teacher gives a long explanation of the material. Then, the teacher says: "Do you understand now?" The student does not understand, but he or she is too embarrassed to admit it. So the student says: "Yes, thanks." The student is eager to leave the office and thinks, "maybe I'll ask one of my friends for a better explanation."

It is important for the teacher to check the listener's understanding at each point. If you are explaining an idea to a student, have the student show you that he or she understands the material by solving a problem or working through an example. You will see this style of teaching in lessons 13-A, 13-B, and 13-C.

Using Pencil and Paper

It may be convenient to use pencil and paper in an office conference. There are several uses for pencil and paper in this setting.

1. If the teacher and the student have a communication problem because of their different language backgrounds, they can often resolve it by writing down the words that are not clear.

2. A diagram on paper may be the best explanation of a concept—a picture is worth a thousand words.

3. The teacher can use paper like a blackboard to write down the main points of an explanation.

4. The teacher can ask the student to solve problems, draw graphs, or write definitions to demonstrate his or her understanding.

Understanding and Using Body Language

For many people, speaking English also means using the body language associated with English. The movements of your body and especially your face can communicate what you are thinking and feeling. Even while you are listening, you may use a combination of facial expressions and other movements to show your reactions.

In an office conference, it may be necessary to listen to a student's problem. If you use appropriate body language while you are listening, the student may feel more comfortable and at ease. The list given below shows some common body movements that often go with the English language. Their meaning is also explained briefly. Keep in mind, however, that body language is very individual, so the items on this chart may not be true for everyone.

Movement	*Meaning*
Eyes on the speaker	I'm listening. I'm interested.
Nodding the head	I understand you. I sympathize with what you say. I agree with you.
Smiling	What you are saying is pleasing, right, or funny.
Eyebrows up	What you are saying surprises me!
Eyebrows together	I have a question about what you are saying. I don't understand what you are saying. What you are saying is strange or upsetting to me.
Leaning forward	I'm trying to understand your point.
Eyes on wristwatch	You're talking too long. I have to go.
Eyes down; eyes sideways	I'm not telling the truth. I'm uncomfortable.
Eyes around the room	I'm bored. I'm thinking about something else.
Eyes staring; face still	I'm angry. I'm hiding my true feelings.
Making sounds during a pause: "uh huh, mm hmm, yeah"	I'm following what you say. I'm interested in what you say.

Have you noticed any other gestures or body movements that seem to occur with the English language?

Body Language and Active Listening*

This is a chance to notice body language among your classmates. Form into groups of three students. In each group, one student is the speaker, one student is the listener, and one student is the reporter. Each student has a special job.

---

*Adapted with permission from Rita Wong, "Learner Variables and Pre-pronunciation Considerations in Teaching Pronunciation," in *Current Perspectives on Pronunciation*, ed. J. Morley (Washington, D.C.: TESOL, 1987).

Speaker: In three minutes, tell the listener about a problem you have had in one of your classes. Just talk naturally.

Listener: Listen actively to what the speaker says. Try to use some of the body language listed above. React naturally with questions, comments, laughter, etc., depending on what the speaker says.

Reporter: Sit so that you are facing the listener. Carefully watch the listener's face. In the space below, make notes on what you see and hear and describe exactly what the listener does and says. When you are finished, report what you saw to the others in your group.

Report about the Listener's Body Language

Body Language   *Sounds (uh huh, etc.)*   *Questions or Comments*

Now, change roles. All three people should get a chance to try each role.

Teachers in Action 1

(Play the videotape "Techniques for Teachers")

Lessons 13-A through 13-C show teachers helping students to understand course material. Notice that in each case, the student is working and thinking hard. All three of these teachers use questions to check that the student understands and learns from the material. Answer the following questions while you watch the videotape.

1. What is the student asking the teacher to do?

    13-A:

    13-B:

    Notice how the teacher summarizes the student's question: "Oh, so you're wondering why is it that sometimes we use 'da' and sometimes there's no 'da' with the 'tomo'?"

    13-C:

2. Is pencil and paper used in the conference? How?

    13-A:

    13-B:

    13-C:

3. Comment on the body language of the people in the conference.

    13-A Teacher:

    13-A Student:

    13-B Teacher:

    13-B Student:

    13-C Teacher:

    13-C Student:

4. Is the student satisfied at the end of the conference? How can you tell?

   13-A:

   13-B:

   13-C:

Fluency Work 1: Using Native Speaker Patterns

The excerpt given below is from lesson 13-A. Play the videotape and do the following activities.

1. <u>Underline</u> the words that receive the most stress and mark pauses with slashes (/).
2. Use arrows ⟋ ⟍ to show rising or falling pitch.
3. Circle the sounds or words that are difficult for you to pronounce.
4. Read the dialogue with a partner. Notice how the teacher never lectures; he explains the material through two-way communication. Practice it several times, trying to get a feel for the interaction between the native speakers on the videotape.

Lesson 13-A

Andy: So, taking this $3x$ squared, um, the first part, 3 is just a constant,

Laura: um hmm

Andy: so you might as well just write down "f prime of x equals" on the next line,

Laura: um hmm, prime of x...

Andy: and, in fact you'd put the prime on the f here.

Laura: OK.

Andy: and cross out the prime under the x. Good. And that stands for the derivative of the function f of x.

Laura: OK.

Andy: The derivative of a power of *x*, say *x* to the *n*,

Laura: um hmm

Andy: is equal to that power *n* times *x* raised to the *n* minus one, that is you bring the power out front

Laura: um hmm

Andy: and then you subtract one and use that for the exponent.

Laura: So squared, subtract one from here?

Andy: um hmm

Laura: So it's 3 just *x* prime?

Andy: To the first power.

Laura: *x* to the first, OK.

Andy: So you could put a one there. And don't forget bringing your power out front also.

Laura: 2, OK, so it's 2 times 3?

Andy: That's right.

Laura: OK, so, 2 times 3 here, so 6*x*.

Andy: Right. And do you know what *x* to the first power is?

Laura: Just the same as *x*.

Andy: Right.

Laura: Right.

Andy: So what's the final answer then?

Laura: Um, 6.

Andy: What happened to your x to the one?

Laura: Um...

Andy: You just told me that x to the one is x.

Laura: Right, so it's $6x$.

Andy: Good. That is the final answer.

Laura: OK.

Andy: Put a box around it.

Laura: Bravo!

Andy: Let's move on to the next one!

Role Play 1: Explaining Material in the Office

Prepare for this role playing by making a lesson plan of a simple concept from your own field.

With another student (ideally from a different field), do a role play of the following situation, using the suggestions given below.

A student comes to your office and says that he or she missed class last week due to illness. He or she asks if you can review your lecture from the class. Using the lesson plan you have prepared, teach the student the lesson.

1. Use appropriate body language. Review the body language section of this unit if you need to.

2. Use questions to check understanding and to help the student think at every step of your explanation.

3. Use pencil and paper if it helps to make things clear.

4. The "student" should ask questions and try to understand.

5. Video- or audiotape your role play.

Self-Evaluation: Role Play I

If your role play was video- or audiotaped, watch or listen to the tape as you fill out this self-evaluation form.

1. What were you trying to explain?

2. List the questions that you asked the student (if you need more space, use a separate page).

3. Were there any points at which you did not understand each other? Describe what happened.

4. By the end of the conference, what had the student learned? How could you tell?

5. List any questions about pronunciation, grammar, or vocabulary.

One on One

Teachers in Action 2

(Play the videotape "Techniques for Teachers")

Lessons 13-D and 13-E show students coming to their teachers with special problems. Play the videotape and answer these questions as you watch.

1. What is the student's problem?

    13-D:

    13-E:

    Notice how the teacher repeats the student's request: "An incomplete? Hmm."

2. What is the teacher's response and the reason for that response?

    13-D:

    13-E:

3. Comment on the body language of the people in the conference.

    13-D Teacher:

    13-D Student:

    13-E Teacher:

    13-E Student:

4. In the end, do you think the student is satisfied? How can you tell?

    13-D:

    13-E:

5. What would you do if you were the teacher in these situations?

    13-D:

    13-E:

Language Models 1: Giving Encouragement

In lesson 13-D, the teacher encourages the student to keep trying hard in the course even though she did poorly on the midterm exam. He uses several techniques to do this. Listed below are three techniques for encouragement and some useful sentences to express encouragement.

1. He gives suggestions for improvement.

    ...what we should do instead is discuss how you can prepare yourself better for taking the final exam.

    So let me recommend that for the next exam you read through the entire exam first and then quickly answer all those that you know right away. And only after you've done that should you go back and answer the harder and longer ones.

    The other thing is there are certain basic skills that you may want to practice a little more, like being faster with the calculator.

    And it may also help you to prepare a review sheet, maybe one or two pages that summarizes everything just to make sure that you can get quickly to that most important material.

    ...and you could save time by writing a shorter answer that would still get you full credit but would then allow you to have some time to answer the later questions.

    There is a study guide that's still available at the bookstore. I think you'll have to be more careful about budgeting your time and to learn certain things about how to take a test efficiently in the amount of time needed.

2. He praises the student for the strong points that she does have.

    Well, based on your homeworks, and what I've seen of your work outside of this exam and also based on your answers to the first few questions, it's clear you do know the material.

    Based on your grades and the homework and on these first few questions, I would say you're doing very well.

    In fact, I think you're one of the better students in the course and I would encourage you to stay in.

3. He says that he will weigh improvement in assigning the final grade.

   Part of my grading policy is, if there's one grade out of the whole course that's out of line, I try and adjust for that so that you would not be penalized unfairly if you do very well on the final.

Language Models 2: Saying "No" Politely

In lesson 13-E, the teacher says "No" to the student's request. However, she tries to be polite in saying "No" so that the student will not become too hurt or angry. Listed below are some of the ways in which she softens the impact of her "No."

1. She uses a polite phrase so that the "no" doesn't sound so strong.

   Gee Tim, I really don't think so.

   I really couldn't accept an incomplete.

2. She tries to present good reasons for her decision so the student will understand her point of view.

   It's just that it's really too late in the quarter to try to do something like that.

   ...because this is a seminar and especially because it's a graduate seminar, the work with your team is so important that it just really, I really couldn't accept an incomplete.

   But you understand my viewpoint?

3. She explains that she would say yes in certain cases. This way, the student will not think she is always so strict.

   Well, you know, that wouldn't be such a problem in a different course, but because this is a seminar....

   If the course were a research course or something where you were working independently, then I could really see doing it better, but it's a course that really depends so totally on your class input and your work with your team members....

Fluency Work 2: Using Native Speaker Patterns

The excerpt given below is from lesson 13-D, in which the teacher is making suggestions to the student about how to improve her performance on exams. Play the videotape and do the following activities.

1. Underline the words that receive the most stress and show pauses with slashes (/).
2. Circle the sounds or words that are difficult for you to pronounce.
3. Read the paragraph out loud. Try it several times until you feel a smooth fluency.

Lesson 13-D

Let me recommend that for the next exam you read through the entire exam first and then quickly answer all those that you know right away. And only after you've done that should you go back and answer the harder and longer ones. And that'll help you get the highest score before the time runs out. Just one more thing: The other thing is there are certain basic skills that you may want to practice a little more, like being faster with the calculator, and it may also help you to prepare a review sheet, maybe one or two pages, that summarizes everything just to make sure that you can get quickly to that most important material.

Fluency Work 3: Speech Analysis

By speaking freely on tape and then analyzing your own speech, you can learn more about the patterns of your language. Follow these steps in analyzing your own speech.

1. Plan some advice and encouragement that you will give to a student.
2. Tape-record your advice and encouragement in your own words; do not read a prepared speech. Spend two minutes or less.
3. Listen to the tape and carefully transcribe your exact words.
4. Make improvements in the grammar, vocabulary, wording, or content if you need to.
5. Mark your transcription to show which words are stressed and where the pauses belong. <u>Underline</u> the stressed words and mark pauses with slashes (/).
6. Circle any words that are difficult to pronounce. Practice these difficult words.
7. Read the passage from your transcription and tape-record it again. Compare the first version to the new version.
8. Put your transcription away, and give the same advice and encouragement again in your own words and tape-record it. Compare this version to the other versions.

Role Play 2: Encouraging Students and Saying "No" Politely

Listed below are some situations in which students come to their teachers with special requests. In each case, the request is difficult to say yes to. Work with a partner and play out each situation, following these suggestions.

1. Listen actively. Try to use appropriate body language.

2. If you say no, be sure to say it politely by using the ideas in this unit. Perhaps you can say yes to part of the request.

3. If you say no, give good reasons for your no.

4. Give the student some encouragement.

5. Video- or audiotape your role play.

1. A student comes to your office. She wants you to raise her grade from the last quiz, saying that there wasn't enough time to finish it. The student knows the material perfectly, but feels that the time was too short to be fair. What will you say?

2. A student comes to your office saying that he missed many of the class lectures and is now behind in the course. The student missed the lectures because he thought the course was easy, and he spent more time on other courses instead. The student now realizes that the material is not so easy. He wants you to tutor him in your office during your spare time, allowing him to catch up in time for the exam. What will you say?

3. A student has a problem with a course conflict. Every Wednesday she has to miss your class because of a lab section in another class. Wednesday is the day you give the weekly quiz. She would like you to give her the quiz early every week in your office. What will you say?

4. A student comes to your office asking to take the final exam early because of a family vacation during final exam period. What will you say?

5. A student comes to your office saying he needs to get a grade of 3.2 in your class in order to get into the Engineering department, and asks if you will raise his scores a bit. You look at your record book. The student has three exam scores so far: 2.5, 2.7, and 3.3. There is still a final exam coming up. You plan to average all four scores for a final grade. What will you say?

Self-Evaluation: Role Play 2

If your role play was video- or audiotaped, watch or listen to the tape as you fill out this self-evaluation form.

1. What did you say to encourage the student?

2. If you said "no," how did you say it politely?

3. Were there any points where you did not understand each other? Describe what happened.

4. By the end of the conference, how do you think your student felt? How can you tell?

5. List any questions about pronunciation, grammar, or vocabulary.

Observation Assignment

1. Observe two Americans having a conversation on campus or in any other public place. Watch the *listener's* body language, especially his or her face. Describe what you see. (If you feel uncomfortable doing this, you can watch from a long distance. You do not need to listen to the conversation. If you still feel uncomfortable, find a conversation that takes place on television or in a movie.)

2. Pay attention to your own body language in conversation. If someone were watching a silent movie of you in conversation, would they know you are not a native speaker of English? Why or why not? Would they know what country you were from? Why or why not?

3. Is your body language different when you talk to native English speakers than when you speak in your own language with friends from your own culture? What differences do you notice?

4. What conclusions can you draw from these observations?

Part IV
Pronunciation

Introduction to Pronunciation

Sound Symbols

The following system is used to represent the sounds in this pronunciation section. Common words are given to indicate which sound is represented.

Consonants

f	foot, father, fast	th	those, this, thing
l	let, last, like	v	vote, very, give
qu	quick, quiet, queen	w	wait, wish, where
r	run, red, right		

Vowels

a	father, stop, clock	I	sit, list, tip
ɔ	call, taught, dog	o	go, slow, no
æ	cat, sat, last	u	too, loose, soon
e	cake, late, day	ʊ	book, would, could
ɛ	set, pen, test	ʌ	but, sun, what
ər	bird, earth, turn	ə	the (same as ʌ)
i	seat, feel, need		

Diphthongs

ai	night, like
au	sound, loud
oi	boy, oil

Pronunciation Strategies

Many nonnative speakers of English complain that, although they can pronounce a certain sound clearly when they try hard, they can not pronounce it clearly when they are speaking

149

freely. If you are in this situation, consider this four-level approach to pronunciation practice using the activities outlined below.

Level 1: Word Level

—Practice the sound in individual words as often as you can.

—Choose certain common words or phrases that contain your problem sounds. Use these common words to practice your sounds every time you say them. For example, if you have trouble with /th/, use the phrase *thank you* for practice. Since you probably say that phrase often in English, you can make a special effort to practice your /th/ every time you say "thank you."

Level 2: Text Level

—Find a written text to read out loud. Choose one particular sound to concentrate on as you read. Go through the text and circle that sound wherever it appears. Read the text out loud and tape-record your reading, paying special attention to the sound. Listen to the tape to assess your pronunciation of that sound.

—Read a written dialogue out loud with a friend. Choose one particular sound to concentrate on as you read. Tape-record the dialogue so you can listen to your pronunciation of that sound.

Level 3: Outline Level

—Make a written outline of something that you would like to say. This time you will be speaking from notes, not reading a written text. Follow the outline as you speak. Speaking like this is more natural than reading, yet not completely free. Choose one particular sound to concentrate on as you speak. Tape-record yourself to hear your pronunciation of that sound.

Level 4: Free Speech Level

—Choose a particular sound to focus on as you speak freely on any topic. Concentrate on that one sound as you speak. Find a friend to listen to you or tape-record yourself to assess your pronunciation.

Unit 14

Consonants

This unit provides suggestions on how to pronounce some of the more difficult consonant sounds in English. Words and dialogues that contain these consonants are included for your practice.

You may want to start individualized word lists for each difficult consonant. At the end of each section is a place to keep a list of common words from your daily life or terminology from your field that contain these consonants. By developing your own personalized word lists, you can remember to practice those words and sounds that are problems for you.

Practice Your Consonants: /th/ *(thin, this)*

To make this sound, place the tip of the tongue between your front teeth. The air flows through the narrow space above the tongue. Look in the mirror: you should be able to see the tip of the tongue between the teeth if you are pronouncing the sound correctly.

This sound may be voiced, made with the vocal cords vibrating, or unvoiced, with the air flowing past the vocal cords. Place your hand on your throat. First pronounce /th/ as in *th*in. You should not feel any vibration because this sound is unvoiced. Now pronounce /th/ as in *th*is. You should feel a vibration in the throat because this sound is voiced. Practice going back and forth between the two sounds with your hand on your throat.

Repeat these words. Ask others if you do not know the meanings.

the	this	there	through	thing	rather	math	north	with
they	that	then	threw	think	bother	bath	south	both

mathematics	author	further	three	333
arithmetic	authority	furthermore	third	3,333
enthusiastic	beneath	otherwise	thirty-three	

eighth	eleventh	thirteenth	length
ninth	twelfth	thirty	width
tenth	thirteen	thirtieth	month

Add your own words to this list.

Dialogues: /th/

Take turns reading these dialogues with a partner. Make an extra effort to pronounce /th/ clearly.

1. *A:* I think the Southwest is the most beautiful place on earth: think of the mountains, the desert, the big sky, the warm weather!

   B: I think the Northwest is the place to be: think of the green trees, the lakes, the ocean, the hills!

   A: Then why do we both live in the East?

2. *A:* How was the exam?

   B: I got a ninety-three.

   A: That's good!

   B: I don't think it's that good.

   A: Ninety-three, not that good?

   B: No. I made all these mistakes in arithmetic. Otherwise I could have gotten the highest grade.

   A: There's another exam next month, isn't there? Check the answers more thoroughly then.

3. *A:* Were you in Math class yesterday?

   B: No, I wasn't there.

   A: Theodore said he thought he saw you there.

   B: Then I think Theodore thought the wrong thing.

   A: Maybe you think he thought the wrong thing, but he thinks he thought the right thing.

   B: I don't think it matters what Theodore thought. The truth is, I wasn't there!

   A: In that case, I think you'd better go to Math on Thursday.

4. *A:* What's the matter? What's that thing on your thumb?

   B: Oh, nothing.

   A: Nothing! You've got a big thick white bandage on your thumb!

   B: Well, the thing is, my brother threw a frisbee to me and it broke my thumb.

   A: And what's the matter with your thigh? Is that another bandage?

   B: Well, yeah, I slipped in the bathtub.

   A: And come to think of it, there's something strange about your voice. Is there a frog in your throat?

   B: No, but I think I got a sore throat from going out in that thunder storm the other night.

   A: Hey, you're really a mess! Are you sure you're still up for the theater tonight?

   B: Of course! I'd rather die than miss the theater!

   A: That's what I was afraid of!

5. *A:* Can I get you something?

   B: Yes, I'd like three of those donuts, thanks.

   A: Which ones, these?

   B: No, those.

   A: These?

   B: No, those, further back.

   A: Oh. These.

   B: No, those, in the fourth row.

   A: Oh, these!

   B: That's right. Those.

   A: OK, here you go. I thought you wanted those others.

   B: No, these are the kind I want.

   A: And you want two of them?

   B: No, three.

   A: One, two, three. That will be $1.35 with tax.

   B: Thank you.

   A: Thank you. Have a nice day!

Idea for Practice: Thank you!

Every time you go shopping, eat in a restaurant, or talk on the phone, you have a chance to say "thank you." Use these chances to practice your /th/ every day.

Consonants: /r/ *(red)*

To produce this sound, curve the sides of the tongue upward so that they press against the insides of the upper teeth. This is a tense sound, so press quite hard in this position. The air flows through the narrow space down the center of the tongue. The tip of the tongue doesn't touch anything. It may turn up or down.

Repeat these words. Ask others for help if you do not know the meanings.

ray	row	rest	right	write	wrist	very	carry	narrow
rate	road	real	wrong	wrote	roast	barrel	merry	early
are	ear	our	far	water	better	sooner	faster	
car	tear	fear	tar	father	wetter	later	slower	
price	free	three	crash	grade	break	try	street	
proud	fresh	threw	crunch	grid	brick	trust	spray	
press	friend	thrust	credit	grind	brunch	tree	scream	

production	radiation	relationship	relativity	crystal
gradually	friction	productivity	thorough	pressure
problems	fraction	practice	digression	credit
shrink	refraction	extreme	concentrate	Friday

Add your own words to this list.

Consonants: /l/ *(let)*

To pronounce this sound, flatten the tongue against the roof of the mouth with the tip of the tongue touching right behind the front teeth. Now curve the sides of the tongue down. The air flows along the sides of the tongue. If you hear the sound /u/ before your /l/, then it means that some air is escaping over the top of the tongue to produce a vowel. Stop that vowel by pushing the center of the tongue harder against the roof of the mouth.

Repeat these words. Ask others for help if you do not know the meanings.

lay	let	last	like	a lot	look	large	battle	tickle
lie	let's	less	low	lock	follow	little	waffle	Hegel

flat	plain	black	class	glad	sleep
flute	please	blue	cloud	glass	slant
fly	play	blow	clue	glide	slight

reflection	apply	elastic	clumsy	eleven
literature	application	elasticity	slightly	family
fluctuate	electricity	California	lightly	local
liable	electrical	inflation	actually	relief

Add your own words to this list.

The Letter *l* at the End of a Word

Words with certain long vowels followed by /l/ sometimes take on a very short extra syllable. Pronounce these words with two syllables:

feel	hail	file	vowel	fuel	foil
meal	mail	trial	towel	rule	coil

Words with short vowels followed by /l/ do not take on an extra syllable. Pronounce these words with one syllable:

| full | fall | hill | tell | dull |
| bull | tall | will | sell | null |

Note these exceptions: /æ/ as in *cat* and /o/ as in *boat* are long vowels, but there is no extra syllable if they are followed by /l/ in a word. Pronounce these words with one syllable.

| pal | bowl |
| Sal | soul |

Dialogues: /r/, /l/

Take turns reading these dialogues with a partner. Make an extra effort to pronounce /r/ and /l/ clearly.

1. *A:* What's wrong? You look depressed.
   B: I feel like I don't have any friends.
   A: But listen, Ruth is your friend, right?
   B: Right, but she just left for Alaska.
   A: Well, isn't Robert your friend?
   B: He left for L.A. last week.
   A: But Ron likes you, right?
   B: Right, but he just left for Raleigh, North Carolina. All my friends are leaving left and right.
   A: You really do have a problem. You have the right to be depressed.
   B: I feel terrible. Horrible.
   A: Well, I'd like to be better friends with you. Let's have lunch this Friday.
   B: Thanks. I'd love to.

2. *A:* What's wrong? You look depressed.
   B: I'm worried about my country. All the letters from my relatives talk about the increasing inflation. Prices are skyrocketing and there are demonstrations in the streets.
   A: What is your government's reaction?

B: Their policies fluctuate from one extreme to the other.

A: I agree that it looks problematic, but worrying won't relieve the region.

B: You're right.

A: Try to get some sleep and concentrate on your course work.

B: I'll try, but it's really hard to be so darn cheerful.

3. *A:* What would you like for breakfast?

   B: I'd like two scrambled eggs, hash browns, and whole wheat toast, please.

   A: Orange juice?

   B: Yes, please.

   A: And will you have coffee this morning?

   B: No, English Breakfast tea, please.

   A: OK. I'll bring your order right away.

4. *A:* Let's get some ice cream!

   B: Great idea! What's your favorite flavor?

   A: Chocolate. Don't you agree?

   B: No, actually, I like the fruit flavors more.

   A: Mmm! That sounds really great!

   B: Let's go stand in line. I'll treat!

Consonants: /w/ *(will)*

To make this sound, round the lips strongly and push them forward. The tongue is in the high-back position. The sound /w/ is usually followed by some vowel.
   Repeat these words. Ask others for help if you do not know the meanings.

would	work	we	where	with	west	one	wear	twelve
wood	wouldn't	when	why	way	western	won	were	twenty
word	while	which	what	away	well	win	wave	twice

Add your own words to this list.

Consonants: /qu/ *(quick)*

This sound is pronounced exactly like /kw/. Form the *k* and then immediately release the air through tightly rounded lips that are pushed forward.
    Repeat these words. Ask others for help if you do not know the meanings.

quick	quality	quantity	question	quotient	equal
quarter	qualify	quantify	equation	quiet	equality
frequent	qualifying exams				

Add your own words to this list.

Consonants: /f/ *(fast)*

To produce this sound, the top teeth rest lightly on the bottom lip. The air flows through the small space between the teeth and lip.
    You should be able to continue this sound for a long time. Place your hand in front of your mouth and feel the air coming out. If you close off the air with the top lip you will pronounce /p/. To avoid this during practice, take your finger and physically push your top lip upward. Now it can not interfere with the sound.

Consonants

Repeat these words. Ask others for help if you do not know the meanings.

fact   fast   fist   for   fill   full   fax   soft   laugh
fall   fun   first   four   Phil   feel   off   tough   cough

field	family	Friday	friction	software
office	familiar	flashcard	function	soften
official	familiarity	defense	football	often
frequency				

Add your own words to this list.

Consonants: /v/ *(vote)*

This sound is produced exactly like /f/, with the top teeth resting lightly on the bottom lip and the air flowing through the small space between the teeth and lip. Unlike /f/, the /v/ sound is voiced. This means that there is vibration in the throat. Put your hand on your throat. Feel the vibration stop and start as you move from /f/ to /v/.

Repeat these words. Ask others for help if you do not know the meanings.

vest   very   verse   vast   van   ever   move   solve   save
verb   every   reverse   village vase   every   prove   resolve drive

vaccine	converse	vertebrate	inverse	vein
vaccination	conversion	invertebrate	inversion	vascular
average	conversation	verify	vibration	vision
vector	value	volume		

Add your own words to this list.

Dialogues: /w/, /qu/, /f/, and /v/

Take turns reading these dialogues with a partner. Make an extra effort to pronounce /w/, /qu/, /v/, and /f/ clearly.

1. *A:* Any questions?

   B: My question is, when is the quiz?

   A: The quiz is Friday. We've had a quiz every Friday all quarter.

   B: Will vectors be on the quiz this week?

   A: Of course! Whatever we study for the week is always on the quiz.

   B: Well, okay! Don't get so worked up, I only asked a question.

2. *A:* I had a fight with a student today.

   B: What happened?

   A: I asked if there were any questions. Then one guy asked when the quiz was.

   B: Well? So what? What's wrong with that?

   A: The answer to that question is obvious. We've had a quiz every Friday all quarter; I was furious at his question.

   B: But students often ask about quizzes.

   A: I know, but this is the seventh week of the quarter and all the quizzes have always been on a Friday.

   B: Did the student figure out that you were miffed?

   A: Yes, unfortunately. I'm afraid my feelings came out in my tone of voice.

   B: Hmm. My advice is to apologize to the fellow as quickly as possible. Otherwise you'll have a bad class atmosphere for the rest of the quarter.

   A: I suppose I'll have to take your advice even though I don't want to.

3. *A:* You look very nice today.

   B: Thank you.

   A: Is that a new vest?

   B: Yes—I don't often wear a vest.

   A: It looks quite distinguished.

   B: I'm glad you think so. I have a job interview this afternoon. I want to convince the interviewers that I'm qualified.

   A: Of course you're qualified. I would hire you right away.

   B: Thanks, but you're my friend. My future boss may not view me in quite the same way.

   A: Are you nervous?

   B: Very!

   A: Don't worry. That vest will win you the job even if you fail in the interview.

   B: Very funny.

4. *A:* What's wrong? You look like death warmed over!

   B: I know. I've been having the worst time getting up for my 7:30 class.

   A: Wow! 7:30 is early! And I know you're used to working until 4:00 or 5:00 in the morning.

   B: It's awful. This morning the alarm went off at 7:00 and I just turned it off and went back to sleep. When I woke up again it was 7:25. I quickly jumped into my clothes and ran all the way to the university.

   A: It's quite close to where you live.

   B: Yeah, but even so I was very late. It was 7:45 when I arrived and I've been a nervous wreck for the rest of the day. Plus now I'm starving because I missed breakfast.

   A: By the way, I'm afraid I have some information that will ruin your day even further.

   B: What?

   A: Your shirt is on backwards and your shoes are on the wrong feet.

   B: Oh no! I've been wearing them this way all day!

   A: It's obviously unfair to offer classes at 7:30.

Unit 15

Vowels

This unit provides suggestions on how to pronounce the vowel sounds of English. The unit begins with a general overview of the English system of vowels as a whole and continues with a specific focus on each vowel. There are words and dialogues that contain these vowels for your practice.

You may want to start individualized word lists for each difficult vowel. At the end of each section is a place to keep a list of common words from your daily life or terminology from your field that contain these vowels. By developing your own personalized word lists, you can remember to practice those words that are problems for you.

Location of Vowels

Each vowel in English is produced with the tongue in one particular part of the mouth, as shown in the illustration. The following activities are designed to help you become familiar with the location of the vowels by actually feeling the movements of the jaws and tongue.

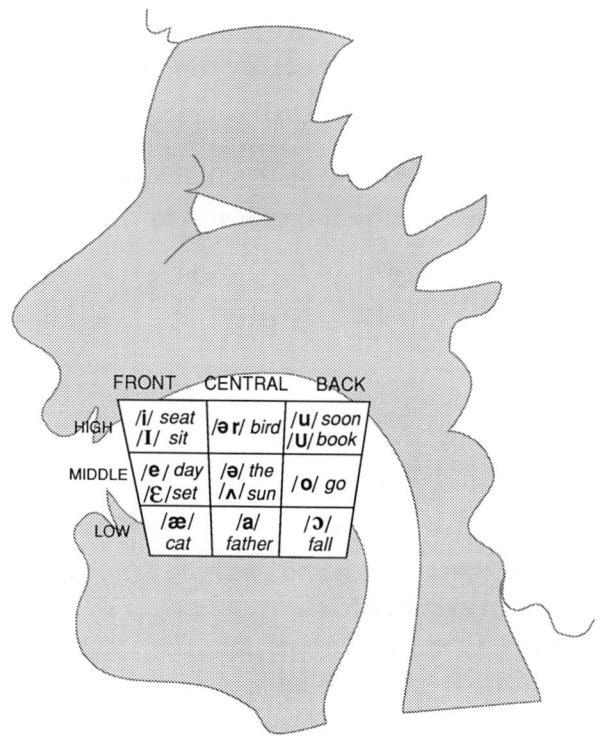

	FRONT	CENTRAL	BACK
HIGH	/i/ seat /I/ sit	/ə r/ bird	/u/ soon /ʊ/ book
MIDDLE	/e/ day /ɛ/ set	/ə/ the /ʌ/ sun	/o/ go
LOW	/æ/ cat	/a/ father	/ɔ/ fall

Location of vowel production

Vowels in the Extreme Positions

The vowels in the most extreme positions of the mouth are:

/i/ (se*a*t)   /u/ (s*oo*n)

/æ/ (c*a*t)   /ɔ/ (f*a*ll)

The vowel /i/ is produced in the highest front part of the mouth.

/i/   *ea*t   *ea*sy   *ea*ch

The next vowel, /æ/ is also produced in the front of the mouth, but in the lowest part.

/æ/   at   as   accident

Feel the jaw and tongue go up and down as you move between these two sounds.

/i/   /æ/   /i/   /æ/   /i/   /æ/

Now move to the lower back of the mouth for /ɔ/. Round the lips slightly.

/ɔ/   ought   all   off

Feel the tongue move backward and forward as you move between these two sounds.

/æ/   /ɔ/   /æ/   /ɔ/   /æ/   /ɔ/

Finally, move to the upper back of the mouth for /u/. Round the lips.

/u/   suit   moon   loop

Feel the jaw and tongue go up and down as you move between these two sounds.

/u/   /ɔ/   /u/   /ɔ/   /u/   /ɔ/

Feel the tongue go forward and back as you move between /u/ and /i/.

/u/   /i/   /u/   /i/   /u/   /i/

You have just practiced the extreme English vowel positions in the mouth. Feel the positions carefully as you move from one sound to the next.

/i/   /æ/   /ɔ/   /u/   /i/   /æ/   /ɔ/   /u/

Switch directions.

/i/   /u/   /ɔ/   /æ/   /i/   /u/   /ɔ/   /æ/

Front Vowels

Now we will locate the vowels that lie between the extremes. There are five vowels that are produced in the front of the mouth.

Place your hands on the sides of your face. Feel your jaw and tongue drop lower and lower as you make each sound in the front of the mouth.

/i/ eat
/ɪ/ it
/e/ ate
/ɛ/ egg
/æ/ at

Back Vowels

There are four vowels that are produced in the back of the mouth.

Place your hands on the sides of your face. Feel the jaw and tongue drop lower and lower as you make each sound in the back of the mouth.

/u/ boot
/ʊ/ book
/o/ boat
/ɔ/ bought

Central Vowels

There are two important central vowels in English, /ʌ/, produced in the exact center of the mouth, and /a/, in the low central position.

Place your hands on the sides of your face. Feel the jaw and tongue go up and down as you move between these sounds.

/ʌ/ cut
/a/ hot

Move the tongue backward and forward among the three horizontal positions, back, central, and front.

/e/ (ate)   /ʌ/ (cut)   /o/ (boat)
/æ/ (at)   /a/ (hot)   /ɔ/ (bought)

There is also a high central vowel that only occurs before /r/. This is the sound in *first* or *word*.

To make this sound, round your lips and begin to form an /r/ sound. The tongue position for the /r/ is very close to the tongue position for the vowel. The vowel sound that comes out as you make the /r/ should be the right one.

    earn   sir   early   word

Diphthongs

Diphthongs are made up of two vowel sounds. English has three:
    /oi/   boy

    /ai/   bite

    /au/   about

To practice these diphthongs, say the two vowel sounds separately and feel the location of each vowel sound. Move them closer and closer together.

o i	a i	a u
o i	a i	a u
o i	a i	a u
oi	ai	au
boy	bite	about

Tense and Relaxed Vowels

English vowels fall into two categories, tense and relaxed. To make a tense vowel, your mouth and face muscles are tight, or tense. To make a relaxed vowel, your mouth and face muscles are relaxed.

In North American English, most speakers exaggerate the length of the tense vowels in stressed syllables. This is why American English sounds a little bit like singing to some people.

Practice adding a strong /y/ to the end of the tense front vowels /i/ and /e/ in the words listed on the following chart. Really stretch the length of the vowel. Then practice adding a strong /w/ to the end of the tense back vowels. Stretch the length of the vowel and round the lips.

	Tense Vowels	Relaxed Vowels
Front Vowels	/i/ (y) eat /e/ (y) ate	/ɪ/ it /ɛ/ egg /æ/ at
Back Vowels	/u/ (w) moon /o/ (w) moan /ɔ/ ought	/ʊ/ put
Central Vowels		/ʌ/ cut /a/ hot
Diphthongs	/ai/ might /au/ out /oi/ boy	

Practice Your Vowels: /i/ *(seat)*

The tongue is in the high front position for this vowel. Tense the mouth and smile when you make this sound. Stretch the sound as if it had a /y/ after it.
  Repeat these words. Ask others for help if you do not know the meanings.

be we see week keep these free peace field

me he she please need three sheet piece feel

equals	Indonesia	immediately	agree	complete
thesis	congeal	compete	agreement	completely
three	thirteen	fifteen	seventeen	nineteen
thirty-three	fourteen	sixteen	eighteen	3,333

Add your own words to this list.

Vowels: /ɪ/ *(sit)*

This front vowel is slightly lower than /i/. Relax the mouth. Feel the jaw and tongue go slightly up and down as you move back and forth from /i/ to /ɪ/. Also, your face muscles should go from tense to relaxed as you move between these two sounds.

Repeat these words. Ask others for help if you do not know the meanings.

bin	this	it	will	him	thin	tip	thing	little
been	miss	is	six	fifth	thick	hint	quick	bit

statistics	probability	continuous	division	six
Indonesia	liquid	friction	decision	sixty-six
civil	interest	invisible	collision	666
limit	literature	dictionary	similar	6,666

Add your own words to this list.

Vowels: /ɪ/ before /r/ *(ear)*

In the word /ear/ the vowel before /r/ is /ɪ/ as in *is,* not /i/ as in *key.* Pronounce the vowel, then tense and curl the tip of the tongue upward as you move into the /r/.

Compare the vowels in the first syllables of these words.

key ring	The /r/ is in a separate syllable; it does not affect the vowel in the word *key.*
earring	The /r/ is in the same syllable as the vowel in *ear;* that vowel is pronounced /ɪ/ as in *it.*

Repeat these words. Ask others for help if you do not know the meanings.

dear   fear   clear   appear   series   experience   material

near   year   beer   mirror   serious   cafeteria   Engineering

Add your own words to this list.

Vowels: /ər/ *(bird)*

This vowel sound does not usually appear by itself. It is a high central vowel that usually comes before /r/. To produce this sound, round the lips and make a very tense mouth. The sides of the tongue are up, touching the sides of the upper teeth. The air flows through the open space along the center of the tongue. The tip of the tongue does not touch anything.

Move back and forth from /ər/ to /ear/. Feel the tongue go backward (/ər/) and forward (/ear/). Feel the lips go from tense (/ər/) to relaxed (/ear/).

Repeat these words. Ask others for help if you do not know the meanings.

her   were   sir   learn   first   worth   word   early   term

work   world   bird   turn   third   hurry   nerd   worm   firm

verge	sooner	circumference	Thursday	thirteen
converge	later	perpendicular	backwards	thirty
converse	better	concern	forwards	percent
service	worse	server	circle	

Add your own words to this list.

Dialogues: /i/, /ɪ/, /ər/, /ear/

Take turns reading these dialogues with a partner. Make an extra effort to pronounce the /i/, /ɪ/, /ear/, and /ər/ sounds clearly.

1. *A:* I heard you were sick.

   B: Yes. I was seriously ill for three weeks.

   A: Three weeks? I can hardly believe it. You poor kid.

   B: I didn't really mind being sick. At least I got some sleep. The worst thing is, I had to quit working on my research for three weeks.

   A: Now that you feel better, it will be easy to get back into it again.

   B: Yes. The trick is to work evenings and weekends until I finish it.

   A: That's ridiculous. If you work evenings and weekends you'll only get sick again!

2. *A:* You're one of the messiest people I've ever seen.

   B: Oh yes, I admit it freely.

   A: Why don't you clean up these sheets of paper?

   B: I don't need to.

   A: Don't you ever feel a need for a little bit of neatness?

   B: Not really.

   A: This is sinful. If your desk were clear you could do some work. Do you think you can find anything here?

   B: Sure, it's easy! If something is missing, I just use your things!

3. *A:* I heard that Kim and Jim had a big disagreement.

   B: Yes. She's concerned with world peace, but he only thinks about his work.

   A: Do you think they'll split up?

   B: Could be. We'll see.

4. *A:* May I please have a beer?

   B: Sure. Here you are.

   A: And could I also have some chips?

   B: Sure. With dip?

   A: Yes, please.

B: Anything else to eat?

A: I don't think so, thanks.

Vowels: /e/ *(day)*

To pronounce this vowel, the mouth is tense. The tongue is in the middle front position. Stretch the length of the sound and pronounce it as if it had a /y/ after it.
  Repeat these words. Ask others for help if you do not know the meanings.

| say | day | make | main | taste | change | today | late | paint |
| may | ray | trade | train | great | planes | lazy | grade | shape |

relationship	container	restatement	eight
graduation	training	maintain	eighty-eight
inflation	TA	maintenance	888
communication	RA	ratio	8,888

Add your own words to this list.

Vowels: ε *(set)*

To produce this vowel, relax the mouth and lower the tongue slightly from /e/. This is a short sound. As you move between /e/ and /ɛ/, the jaw and tongue should go down and up slightly, and the face muscles should go from tense to relaxed.
  Repeat these words. Ask others for help if you do not know the meanings.

| met | let | next | says | yes | any | every | ready | guess |
| get | bet | text | said | best | many | never | head | then |

necessary	Mexico	exercise	question	ten
necessity	second	registration	professor	eleven
successful	chemistry	speciality	relative	777
medicine	engineering	section	Wednesday	7,710
economics				

Add your own words to this list.

Vowels: /æ/ (sat)

To produce this vowel, smile and open the mouth. The mouth and face muscles are relaxed, and the tongue is in the low front position.
   Repeat these words. Ask others for help if you do not know the meanings.

mad	bad	cat	ask	class	fact	task	answer	gram
sat	man	can't	that	graph	gas	have	pass	fast

maximum	capacity	program	masters	subtract
actually	attraction	Saturday	mandatory	natural
mathematics	management	collapse	strategy	transfer
random	sample	example	Japan	

Add your own words to this list.

Vowels: /ɛ/ before /r/ *(air)*

Both /e/ and /ɛ/ are pronounced /ɛ/ before an /r/ in the same syllable. In the word *air* the vowel before /r/ is /ɛ/ as in *men,* not /e/ in *day.* Note the difference between the vowels in these words:

mayor   The /e/ is in a separate syllable from the /r/; it is pronounced /e/ as in *day.*

mare   The vowel is in the same syllable with the /r/; it is pronounced /ɛ/ as in *men.*

Repeat these words. Ask others for help if you do not know the meanings.

tear air fair where there area hilarious secretary
care scare dare marry their pair terrible cherry

Add your own words to this list.

Dialogues: /e/, /ɛ/, and /æ/

Take turns reading these dialogues with a partner. Take special care to pronounce the vowels /e/, /ɛ/, and /æ/ clearly.

1. *A:* I'm fed up with my graduate program. I quit.
   B: Wait! What about your grades? What about graduation?
   A: I don't care. I'm not enthusiastic.
   B: Don't say that. You scare me to death.

2. *A:* I wanted to be successful on the test so I asked Jane for help.
   B: What did she say?
   A: She said, "No, take care of your own test!"
   B: Americans are too competitive.
   A: No, Jane is just an extra competitive person.

3. *A:* My professor and I are working together on a project.

   B: A special opportunity for you?

   A: No, for the professor. Everyone knows that sometimes RAs do most of the work but the professor's name is on the publication.

4. *A:* Next Wednesday is a question and answer session in our quiz section.

   B: Should I attend?

   A: Yes. Definitely. Otherwise I'll just have to lend you my notes later.

5. *A:* What is your major?

   B: Mathematics. And you?

   A: Chemistry.

   B: Too bad. We'll never understand each other.

6. *A:* My friend is attracted to our department secretary.

   B: Can he ask her out?

   A: Maybe, but I'm afraid there's a snag.

   B: A snag?

   A: She's married.

   B: What a drag.

7. *A:* Do you exercise?

   B: Yes. I jog around the track every day.

   A: You must be in great shape!

   B: No, I'm ready to collapse.

8. *A:* My memory is failing.

   B: That's terrible.

   A: Yesterday I forgot where I left my backpack and then I forgot my own address!

   B: Maybe you should go to the Health Center.

   A: I forgot where it is.

   B: Graduate students have too much stress.

9. *A:* What time do you usually go to bed?

   B: Bed? What's that? I haven't slept since last September.

   A: Graduate students have way too much stress.

Vowels: /u/ *(too)*

For this vowel, the tongue is in the high back position. To pronounce it, round the lips and tense the mouth, stretching the length of the sound. Add a /w/ to the end.
  Repeat these words. Ask others for help if you do not know the meanings.

| to | two | do | soon | new | suit | view | food | rude |
| too | true | due | moon | knew | through | review | mood | you |

volume	book review	institution	university	produce
vacuum	conclude	opportunity	newspaper	202
communication	conclusion	consumer	usually	2,202
uniform	Tuesday	reduce	intrude	

Add your own words to this list.

Vowels: /ʊ/ *(book)*

For this vowel, the tongue is also in the high back position. To pronounce it, round the lips slightly and relax the mouth. Lower the jaw and tongue slightly from /u/ as in *moon*, but keep it far in the back. This is usually a short sound.
  Repeat these words. Ask others for help if you do not know the meanings.

| book | wood | should | took | shook | full | cook | stood |
| look | would | could | put | good | pull | push | understood |

Add your own words to this list.

Vowels: /ʌ/ (sun)

This sound is produced with the tongue right in the center of the mouth. Relax the mouth completely. It is a short sound. Note that this sound is very close to /ə/. In unstressed syllables, many vowels are pronounced this way; for example, *the*.

Repeat these words. Ask others for help if you do not know the meanings.

| luck | must | bus | trust | thus | sun | done | come | want |
| what | much | was | fund | does | son | one | lunch | just |

pulse	production	construction	consult	Monday
comfort	reduction	destruction	consulting	refund
comfortable	result	construct	culture	one hundred
uncomfortable	repulse	multicolor	something	unjust

Add your own words to this list.

Dialogues: /u/, /ʊ/, and /ʌ/

Take turns reading these dialogues with a partner. Make an extra effort to pronounce /u/, /ʊ/, and /ʌ/ clearly.

1. *A:* Want to go to the lunchroom?

    B: No. Usually the food is no good there. Plus, it costs too much.

    A: Look, I'll lend you some money. Just come.

    B: What for? I don't want to.

    A: But I have a crush on one of the cooks!

2. *A:* What were the results of your study?

    B: I'm not in the mood to discuss my study.

    A: What? Something wrong?

    B: I asked twenty-one subjects to come to room 100, but only one showed up. The others misunderstood and went to the wrong room.

    A: What bad luck. I wonder what you should do.

    B: Just now I should eat some good food. Come on.

3. *A:* What's the trouble?

    B: I have too much to do. I have 202 things to do.

    A: Should I help you? Would it be useful if I took your books back for you?

    B: Wonderful!

    A: And I could stop at the food store for you.

    B: Thanks very much. Now I only have 200 things to do!

4. *A:* Do you take the bus to school?

    B: No. I usually drive my truck.

    A: Isn't it unusual for a student to own a truck?

    B: Maybe so, but I work for a construction company after school every Tuesday. The truck belongs to the company.

    A: And the company trusts you to use their truck?

    B: Sure they trust me. It's my brother's company, you see.

    A: What good luck!

5. *A:* What would you like for lunch?

   B: I'll have one egg sunny side up and one English muffin. And tell the cook to rush it.

   A: But it's one o'clock. Now we only serve lunch foods.

   B: What bad luck. I'm not in the mood for lunch. I just woke up!

6. *A:* I have never understood the customs of lunch and brunch.

   B: One comes sooner than the other, so it just depends on what time you get up.

   A: Which one comes sooner, lunch or brunch?

   B: Brunch. If you wake up late you can have brunch instead of breakfast. What time do you usually wake up?

   A: 1:30 or 2:00 P.M.

   B: Uh oh! Then you've missed both brunch and lunch! You'd better wait for supper.

   A: All this talk about lunch, brunch, supper, cooking, and good food makes me hungry!

Vowels: /o/ *(go)*

To produce this sound, round and tense the lips with the tongue in middle back position. Stretch the sound. Put a /w/ after the sound.
   Repeat these words. Ask others for help if you do not know the meanings.

| Oh! | so | no | open | over | old | loan | cold | boat |
| go | toe | know | close | own | mold | low | row | note |

| microscope | zoology | tomorrow | vocation | control |
| telescope | noticeable | notation | prodrug | rotate |

Add your own words to this list.

Vowels: /o/ before /r/ *(or)*

To make this sound, produce an /o/ and then move the tongue forward into the /r/ position. The lips stay rounded for both sounds.
   Repeat these words. Ask others for help if you do not know the meanings.

| warm | or | sorry | four | north | order | orientation | portion |
| warn | for | war | 444 | boring | form | northern | formula |

Add your own words to this list.

Vowels: /ɔ/ *(fall)*

To make this sound, round the lips and tense the mouth with the tongue in the low back position. Stretch the length of the sound and put a /w/ at the end. This vowel is often spelled with an *o*. Note that many U.S. speakers of English pronounce this sound like /a/, as in *father*. You may do so too.
   Repeat these words. Ask others for help if you do not know the meanings.

| awe | law | talk | all | boss | often | caught | small | long |
| saw | raw | walk | call | dog | offer | taught | tall | wrong |

office	automatic	because	protocol	Tylenol
officer	autocratic	always	installment	causation
author				

Add your own words to this list.

Vowels: /a/ *(father)*

To produce this vowel, relax the mouth completely and drop the jaw slightly with the tongue in low central position.
   Repeat these words. Ask others for help if you do not know the meanings.

hot	a lot	father	lock	top	non	box
not	dot	crops	rock	bottom	stop	plot

biology	technology	concentrate	oscillate	logical
psychology	technological	opportunity	contact	policy
astronomy	botany	contract		

Add your own words to this list.

Vowels: /a/ before /r/ *(art)*

To make this sound, produce an /a/ and then move the tongue upward into the /r/ position. If you have trouble with this sound, try putting a word that begins with /r/ after a word that ends with /ar/, for example, *car ride*. Link these words together so that there is one /r/. Feel your mouth movements as you make the /r/. Can you keep that /r/ sound on *car* when you remove the word *ride*?
   Repeat these words. Ask others for help if you do not know the meanings.

far	start	architecture	arc	hardly
farm	art	seminar	arctic	part
bar	artistic	department	arch	particle
car	smart	departure	argument	market

Add your own words to this list.

Dialogues: /o/, /a/, and /ɔ/

Take turns reading these dialogues with a partner. Make an extra effort to pronounce /o/, /ɔ/, and /a/ clearly.

1. *A:* My office mate never stops talking all day long. I can hardly concentrate.

    B: Talk to your boss about it.

    A: Impossible.

    B: Why?

    A: My office mate is my boss!

2. *A:* Let's go to the architecture department.

    B: Why? My department is biology.

    A: But the architecture department has a coffee shop in the north part of the building.

    B: OK. Let's get going!

3. *A:* This homework problem is not logical.

    B: That's because you're holding it wrong. Here. This is the bottom and this is the top.

    A: Oh no! It was upside-down.

    B: Graduate students have too much stress.

4. *A:* Do you own a car?

    B: Yes.

    A: Could I possibly borrow it?

    B: No. Sorry. It broke a week ago.

    A: So, get it fixed.

    B: Impossible. I'm also broke!

5. *A:* So, how's your project going?

   B: Oh, I don't know. Pretty slow.

   A: It's your own fault. You spend too much time on your English course.

   B: I know, but my English course is so marvelous that I can't stop working on it and I ignore my departmental responsibilities.

   A: Control yourself. You have to get organized.

Appendixes

Appendixes

Appendix 1

Discussions on American Culture

Listed below are several topics for discussion on American culture. Discuss them as a class or in small groups. If you are using this workbook for self-study, you may find that these discussion questions are good conversation topics. Try raising these questions with other members of your department.

Discussion 1: Teaching Styles

1. What is "teaching style"? Decide on a definition.
2. From the videotape "Techniques for Teachers" and from your own classes, you have been exposed to several teaching styles. Describe some of the teaching styles you have seen.
3. How do students react to different teaching styles?
4. Is there a North American teaching style? How is it different from other countries?

Discussion 2: Undergraduate Students

1. In the United States, university student populations are becoming more diverse, especially at the undergraduate level. Discuss the differences you have noticed among undergraduates on your campus.
2. On the other hand, most undergraduates have certain things in common. List what they have in common. Would the same list apply to undergraduate students in other parts of the world?
3. Why do undergraduates go to college? List all the reasons you can think of.
4. For those who are teaching: consider the undergraduates you have in class. What do they expect from you as a teacher? What kind of a relationship do you have with them?
5. This is a true story.

    For several years my friend Doug was teaching astronomy at a small private college.

Now he has a job teaching at a large state university where he finds a surprising difference. Instead of their parents' paying the bills, most of the students work to support themselves, so they have very little extra time for studying. They want to know exactly what they have to do to pass a course and nothing more. Doug finds it frustrating to teach them because they don't have time to enjoy learning for its own sake.

Is this situation familiar to you? Do you have any advice for Doug?

Discussion 3: Your Department

1. Put together some statistics about your department and then compare them with others.

    Who is the chair? How many full, associate, and assistant professors are there? Do you know what these terms mean?

    How many graduate students are there? Where are they from?

    How many TA and RA positions are there?

    How many people are on the office staff?

    Where does the major funding for your department come from?

2. Why did you choose this particular department?

3. Do you understand what tenure is? Do other countries have this system? What is your opinion about this system?

4. Is there any social life in your department? Describe it to other students. Do you participate yourself?

Discussion 4: Time for Work

1. What is your position in your department? How much work do you have to do? Compare this with others in different departments.

2. Many people say that the work load for a student in the United States is much heavier than it is in other countries. Do you agree? Why or why not? How about the work load for professors?

3. This is a true story.

    Maia, a student from Indonesia, had a particular problem. It was near the end of the quarter and she had two important exams coming up. She was also a grader for a course with more than 100 final exams to grade. On top of that, she had research to do for a project with her professor. What a lot of work! Suddenly, she got a letter from her boyfriend saying that he was coming fom Indonesia during the last two weeks of the quarter, with his parents and sister. She would be expected to cook for them and entertain them while they were in the United States. They would all be staying in her small apartment.

What should she do?

Discussion 5: Respect for the Teacher

This is a true story.

A graduate student from China was teaching a quiz section once a week. Attendance in his class was rather poor. Students arrived late and sometimes they did not come at all. Some students came in, asked one or two specific questions, and then left when they had the answers they needed. They did not even wait until the end of class to leave.

In small groups or as a class, discuss the issue of respect for the teacher.

1. This particular teacher felt that the students did not respect him. Do you think his perception was correct?

2. What is respect? How do students show respect for teachers in North America? In other parts of the world?

3. What would you do if you were the teacher in this situation? What options does this teacher have?

4. What are the students' reasons for poor attendance? List all the possible reasons you can think of for their behavior.

Discussion 6: Universities around the World

1. Compare university life in different countries that you are familiar with.

2. Where does the money come from to pay for student tuition and expenses in other countries? In this country?

3. Compare the relationship between students and faculty here and in other countries. How is the relationship between faculty and office staff? Between students and office staff? How do undergraduates differ from graduates in their departmental relations?

4. A "dress code" is a rule about what a person may wear to work. Is there a dress code at your institution for undergraduates? For graduate students? TAs? Professors? Office staff? Are there dress codes in other countries?

Discussion 7: Tests and Exams

1. Make a list of all the different types of exams you can think of that are used in North Amercian universities.

2. If you are teaching, how many exams will you give this quarter or semester? What kind of exams are they?

3. If you are a graduate student, you probably have to take general exams, oral exams, qualifying exams, etc. Describe the exams in your department to other students.

4. What is your opinion about the exam system in this country?

5. What is the attitude toward cheating on exams in your department? At your university? In this country? In other countries? What would you do if you suspected one of your students of cheating?

Appendix 2

"Teachers in Action" Transcripts

Unit 1: Introductions

Lesson 1-A

Andy: Hello and welcome to the second class of Math 105, Introduction to Calculus. In our last lecture we covered the administrative details of the course and reviewed the background concepts. Are there any questions at this point before we get started with our main material for the quarter?

We're now ready to begin our study of the differential calculus and we'll begin with today's topic, the derivative. We're all intuitively familiar with the idea of a derivative. It is simply a rate of change. We'll be talking about the mathematics of how one thing changes as another things change, as another thing changes, we will define this concept, we'll give examples of it, and we'll show you how to work problems with it. That's our purpose today.

Lesson 1-B

June: We have a single page handout today which has 4 graphs on it that we'll be talking about during the course of today's lecture. The topic for today is the idea of correlation. We can look at the word correlation and see that it's really made up of two parts: *co*, meaning together. You've seen that part of a word in words like *cooperation*, *coworkers*. And *relation*. So we're gonna look at the relation together of two variables. We're gonna look at the correlation between two variables.

What we'll be looking at today is, first of all, what we mean by the statistical concept of correlation and then later on what we'll look at is an actual statistic; a number that we can compute from a set of data which measures the strength of correlation between two variables.

Let's begin. I think the best way to begin is by looking at some examples.

Lesson 1-C

Daphne: In the last couple of weeks in this class we've focused on sort of the global aspects of international marketing. We've talked about things that promote trade, things that inhibit trade, like trade barriers versus agree, trade agreements, and economic conditions that make it difficult to operate internationally. Today we're going to focus on the product and taking a product abroad and then this is going to lead into our discussion, a little bit later in the course, on pricing, and distribution, and promotion. So, for today...

Unit 2: Transitions

Lesson 2-A

Andy: At this point we've completed our definition and given one example. Before we move along to a more general interpretation of the derivative, are there any questions at this point? Yes, Doug?

Doug: I'm a little confused about *h*. It, what, what does it have to do with anything here. It seems to disappear.

Andy: The question is, what is the role of *h* in the definition of the derivative. Because it doesn't appear in the answer, what is it doing there. Let me put the formula back up and draw you a picture that'll show you what it's doing there.

Lesson 2-B

Andy: So we've actually computed an example of a derivative from first principles, verified from drawing a picture that it makes intuitive sense. Yes?

Doug: Ah, the curve seems to get steeper on both sides of zero. How does that come out in the formula?

Andy: The question is, the curve is getting steeper on both sides—how is that reflected in the formula for the derivative. The answer is clear...

Lesson 2-C

June: And this one is again positive. Great. Very good.

So now we have some idea about the direction of correlation, positive or negative. We can also look at strength of correlation, the degree of correlation. One of the things we can tell by looking at these plots is for these three plots that have...

Lesson 2-D

Andy: Next what I'd like to do is work a mathematical example, and show you how you would actually compute a derivative. So far we have given a formal definition and shown some of the intuition behind it, but so far we have not actually calculated one. Let me do that in a straightforward case.

Lesson 2-E

Andy: And there's a completed problem, involving derivatives, involving fallen, falling objects from physics.

I have two more general applications to mention to you. The next is from vocabulary. If you imagine...

Lesson 2-F

Andy: ...is how quickly new words are being acquired by that person. Final, general application, um, the derivative is used a lot in economics. There's something economists call a marginal cost. That's defined as the extra cost of producing one more object in a factory...

Lesson 2-G

June: Let's begin, I think the best way to begin is by looking at some examples. So refer first of all to the upper right-hand plot on your handout. This particular plot depicts data from the results of a study on hybridization of two different closely related species of ducks, the mallard and the pintail. And the question that was being addressed by this particular study is whether crossbreeds, so ducks that have a one mallard parent and one pintail parent, if you look at them, and you notice that a particular duck looks more like the pintail parent that it does like the mallard parent, is it also true that its behavioral charact— behavioral characteristics will be more like the pintail.

So what we have here is we have a scale, where the appearance of the duck is rated on a scale from zero actually all the way up to twenty (we only observe values between four and sixteen), and we've also got observations on the behavior of ducks, scaled in the same way; smaller values correspond to being more like like a mallard, larger values correspond to being more like a pintail and we have this particular scatter plot.

What can we see? When you make a plot of two variables, what you want to do is stand back away from your plot and look at its basic shape. When I look at this plot I see a cloud of points that is basically oval in shape with the oval pointing from lower left to upper right. That means to me that ducks that had a higher plumage rating tended also to have a higher behavioral rating. Ducks that had a lower plumage rating tended also to have a lower behavioral rating.

Let's skip for right now onto the next plot, the plot that's labeled demographics on your handout. And this particular plot depicts data, ah, from various countries. We have on the horizontal axis, the percentage, the percentage of economically active women in each of these countries, and on the vertical axis, we have the crude birth rate. If we step away from this plot now and look at its basic shape, I see a plot which is again roughly oval in shape. This time the oval has the opposite orientation; it's going from upper left to lower right.

The third plot that we have, the one that's labeled baseball on the lower left-hand corner of your handout, were collected to investigate the question as to whether American league baseball teams which are at higher altitudes, whose home parks are at higher altitudes, tend to score more home runs, um, the theory being that if you're at a higher altitude, the air is thinner and therefore the ball will go further and so we have here the 1972 figures from the American league, and if we stand back away from this plot and look for its basic shape, well, we'd like to see it being nice and oval shaped, but actually I see it being just a big nebulous cloud of points with no particular pattern to it. So whereas we saw with the ducks and with the demographics that if I told you something about the value of the variable that was on the horizontal axis, you could probably tell me something about the value of the variable on the vertical axis, whereas for the baseball set of data, knowing the altitude of the ball park really doesn't tell me very much about how many home runs I would have expected from that particular team.

Well, let's look now at the fourth plot. The final plot for today's lecture depicts prices of houses in a particular small town, plotted against the square footage as a measure of the size of the house. What do you see in this plot?

Andrew: As square footage increases, so does the price.

June: As square footage increases, so does the price. Definitely. When we have higher values of square footage, we also have higher values of price. How would you describe the basic shape of this plot?

Andrew: A line?

June: It's pretty close to a straight line, not exactly a straight line, I'd actually say it's again oval, but a skinny oval. Much skinnier than the other ovals that I've drawn.

Unit 3: Restating and Summarizing

Lesson 3-A

Andy: That derivative is defined as notation f prime of x equals, the limit, as an auxiliary variable that's just in there temporarily, goes to zero, of the ratio of how much f changes, that's f of (x plus h) minus f of x, with respect to how much x itself is changed by moving from x to (x plus h). That ratio, in the limit, for very very small h, that gives us the instantaneous rate of change, defines the derivative. That concept is important so let me write it down for you and say it again; this derivative gives us the instantaneous rate of change of the function f with respect to the variable letter x. Let me give an example...

Lesson 3-B

Andy: The limit as h tends to zero will have a line that's exactly tangent to the curve. Just like this one is. This is the tangent line, and the fact is, the slope of the tangent line is the same as the derivative. That's an important idea. The slope of this tangent line equals the derivative f prime of x. Any time you hear the word derivative, think in your mind, if you had a graph of that function, we're talking about how steep that is, that is, the curve is steeper here, it has a steeper tangent, and the derivative is measuring the steepness of the curve there. So I hope I've answered your question...

Lesson 3-C

Andy: ...giving us $32x$ as the derivative—remember what a derivative is: it's the rate of change. In particular, rate of change of distance with respect to time is a speed. So this is now giving us the speed in feet per seconds after any amount of time. After x seconds. As you know if you've ever jumped a moderately large distance...

Lesson 3-D

June: It's called the correlation coefficient. The correlation coefficient in standard notation is just denoted lower case r, and it measures the linear relationship between two variables, so the correlation coefficient measures the strength of a linear relationship between two variables.

Lesson 3-E

Daphne: And the most important thing to think about when making design or, or product decisions and changes is, what's the consumer willing to pay for? That's really the underlying question. What are they willing to pay for? So, not only what need does it satisfy, but what are they willing to pay for?

Lesson 3-F

Andy: Next what I'd like to do is work, ah, a mathematical example and show you how you would actually compute a derivative. So far we've given a formal definition and shown some of the intuition behind it, but so far we have not actually calculated one. Let me do that in a straightforward case.

Lesson 3-G

Andy: So we've actually computed an example of a derivative from first principles, verified from drawing a picture that it makes intuitive sense.

Lesson 3-H

June: So, so far we've looked at four plots. We've seen that two of them have basically oval shapes. So we have oval-shaped pointing upward; that would describe the ducks and the houses. We've got an oval-shaped plot which is pointing downward; which is the demographics plot, and we also have the baseball plot which is really basically a round plot, or a plot with no particular pattern—with no clear orientation.

So the first plot, the oval shape pointing upward, look like this, oval-shaped pointing downward, look like this, and round are just round.

Lesson 3-I

Andy: Any other questions at this point? Let me summarize what we've done today: we've concentrated on learning about the derivative; we've given its definition; we've learned what that definition means in terms of a graph; we've worked through an example, and perhaps most importantly to people in applied studies, we've learned how to interpret that derivative as a rate of change. It's how quickly is something changing with respect to something else, as a speed is, for example. We've also learned that it's the slope of the tangent line, and it expresses how steep the curve is at any given point, as a curve is rather, um, level, the slope is nearly zero, as it heads upward it has a large derivative, a large slope. Then it might level off and have a smaller derivative again. The derivative is at any time, always expressing that rate of change: how quickly are things changing, changing in the vertical sense where it's making large changes over a small region in here, very small changes in other places. And finally we've seen examples from physics, from economics, and there are many many other examples in other fields.

Lesson 3-J

June: Well, next lecture, we'll see exactly how you compute this statistic, *r,* this correlation coefficient, for a set of data. We'll actually go through the formulation, ah, and the computation for the statistic.

So let's step back and look at what we've talked about. We've looked at scatter diagrams: ways of depicting two variables of data, we've looked at their basic shapes and we've seen three particular basic shapes. We've seen the oval pointing upward, the oval pointing downward, and the round scatter diagram, so we've seen three basic shapes. Ah, we've noticed that when you look at a scatter diagram, you can see, not only the direction of correlation, but the degree of association. More highly associated variables have skinnier scatter diagrams. We've also learned that there is a statistic called the correlation coefficient, which statisticians denote by the letter *r,* which measures the strength of association between two variables. And next time we'll learn how to compute it. So are there any questions?

Unit 4: Definitions

Lesson 4-A

June: This particular plot depicts data from the results of a study on hybridization of two different closely related species of ducks, the mallard and the pintail. And the question that was being addressed by this particular study is whether crossbreeds, so ducks that have a one mallard parent and one pintail parent, if you look at them . . .

Lesson 4-B

Andy: The exact definition of this derivative is as follows: The derivative of a function *f* of *x*—that's something that gives us a value for every possible value of *x*—that derivative is defined as notation *f* prime of *x* equals the limit as an auxiliary variable that's just in there temporarily, goes to zero of the ration of how much *f* changes, that's *f* of (*x* plus *h*) minus *f* of *x* with respect to how much *x* itself is changed by moving from *x* to (*x* plus *h*). That ratio in the limit for very very small *h,* that gives us the instantaneous rate of change, defines the derivative.

Lesson 4-C

Andy: Final, general application: um, the derivative is used a lot in economics. There's something economists call a marginal cost. That's defined as the extra cost of producing one more object in a factory, ignoring all the fixed costs, maybe it costs two million dollars to build the factory, but to turn out one more recording of your favorite rock and roll star, maybe that only costs fifty or seventy-five cents. It's that marginal cost, the extra cost of producing one unit, that's very important in many kinds of economic analysis, that marginal cost.

Lesson 4-D

June: The topic for today is the idea of correlation. We can look at the word correlation and see that it's really made up of two parts: *co,* uh, meaning together. You've seen that part of a word in words like *cooperation, coworkers.* And *relation.* So we're gonna look at the relation together of two variables. We're gonna look at the correlation between two variables. What we'll be looking at today is, first of all what we mean by...

Lesson 4-E

June: So we'd like to come up with a statistic or some measure, which describes the degree of clustering about the line and we do, as statisticians, have a statistic: it's called the correlation coefficient. The correlation coefficient in standard notation is just denoted lower case *r,* and it measures the linear relationship between two variables. So the correlation coefficient measures the strength of a linear relationship between two variables.

Lesson 4-F

June: When we look at plots and we notice that we have basically an oval-shaped scatter diagram pointing upwards, we say that the scatter plot, scatter diagram is depicting positive correlation. So here we've got positive correlation, or we can say that the two variables, plumage and behavior, are positively correlated. If the scatter diagram is pointing downward, we say we've got negative correlation and if we're in the third case and we have a round nebulous cloud of points with no clear orientation, pretty much what we can say about the correlation is that there is very little or perhaps no correlation.

Lesson 4-G

Daphne: Now, the other thing that you can think about, though, are functional features. And, um, we just talked about some of those things, uh, the primary function, for the bicycle in, in the U.S., versus the bicycle in China is completely different. In the U.S., the primary function really for most bicycle users is for pleasure, or for sports, exercise. The primary function of a bicycle in China is, of course, transportation, so that primary function is different and of course, secondary functions might be different also. Can you think of any examples of what, you know, sort of a secondary function might be?

Barbara: In China, or in the States?

Daphne: Either.

Barbara: Uh huh, well, transportation in a way is secondary here, isn't it?

Daphne: OK, so...

Barbara: ...to recreation.

Daphne: Yeah, so that would be a secondary function here, uh huh. I think that another thing might be, um, well, in China for example, carrying things, um, you would definitely need a basket. You're either carrying other, you know, children or you're carrying, um, groceries home, things like that, so that that affects the basic design of your product, if you're going to need to, to make the bike stable with heavy things on the back, you know, obviously...

Bob: Functional features: do you mean additional features to the bike?

Daphne: A feature that affects the way it's used, yeah, the way it functions. So that if it functions to carry, um, groceries and things like that then it has to have certain attributes just because of that function. OK? The third thing to think about...

Unit 5: Examples

Lesson 5-A

Andy: Um, for example, let the function f represent the distance from Seattle at a given time x.

So for each amount of time—half an hour, one hour, two hours, as you're driving away from the city—the function f of x simply records your odometer in your car; how many miles from Seattle you are. Let's suppose you start off, um, at initially in Seattle, so you're zero miles away, and one hour later, f of one tells you you're 50 miles from Seattle. Now you could say you're 50 miles away in one hour, that's 50 miles per hour, that would almost be a derivative. That would be this ratio before taking the limit. That would be the average rate of change. The derivative itself is related to that but is the instantaneous rate of change of that function, rather than giving you the average rate of change, average speed over the entire hour, the derivative f prime at any time x gives you your speed at that time.

There are many different ways you could travel 50 miles in one hour. You could spend that hour going 50 miles an hour, or you could sit there for half an hour not moving at all at zero miles per hour and then go 100 miles an hour for the next half hour (if you didn't get caught). Your average speed would still be 50 miles per hour. However, your derivative, your instantaneous rate of speed, could be quite different along the way in those two cases.

Lesson 5-B

Andy: The next is from vocabulary. If you imagine children learning words over time and you let the function f of x represent the number of words that they know at age x—generally speaking, young children learn words, learn more and more words—that's an increasing function. The derivative of that function is the rate of change of number of words with respect to time. It's how quickly the child is learning new words.

You could have two children, one of which knows a lot more words than the other; that would be just the function f itself; what the derivative is measuring is how quickly new words are being acquired by that person.

Lesson 5-C

Andy: I have one more specific example for you today. This example is from physics, and concerns how fast an object falls when you drop it—for example, an eraser to the floor....

Lesson 5-D

June: The third plot that we have, the one that's labeled baseball in the lower left-hand corner of your handout, were collected to investigate the question as to whether American league baseball teams which are at higher altitudes, whose home parks are at higher altitudes, tend to score more home runs, um, the theory being that if you're at a higher altitude, the air is thinner and therefore the ball will go further and so we have here the 1972 figures from the American league, and if we stand back away from this plot and look for its basic shape, well, we'd like to see it being nice and oval shaped, but actually I see it being just a big nebulous cloud of points with no particular pattern to it. So whereas we saw with the ducks and with the demographics that if I told you something about the value of the variable that was on the horizontal axis, you could probably tell me something about the value of the variable on the verticle axis, whereas for the baseball set of data, knowing the altitude of the ball park really doesn't tell me very much about how many home runs I would have expected from that particular team.

Lesson 5-E

Daphne: Well, I think that one, one thing that you see often in examples like Japan, if they're trying to sell kitchen appliances, for example, um they, they might have, have done a little research to find out what need it satisfied. A food processor, Cuisinart would do really well if you think of how much chopping is involved in, in Japanese cooking, but the other thing that you have to consider is what are they willing to pay for and if you have a very small kitchen, do you really want a Cuisinart when you could just have a knife. So, yeah, that's, that's been a problem.

Um, what else? What other things can you think of . . .

Unit 6: Graphs and Diagrams

Lesson 6-A

Andy: Let's apply this graph to the example we did just a moment ago. When you carefully plot the function x to the sixth power, you find something that rises very steeply on both sides. Because it's an even power, you get a positive number even when *x* is a negative number because it's multiplying by itself. The derivative here of 6*x* to the fifth: what is that derivative when *x* is zero? Class?

Ann: Zero?

Andy: Right. When you plug in zero for *x*, you get a derivative of zero. Here at *x* equals zero, here at the origin, we verify that the tangent line is indeed horizontal, that is to say, it has a slope of zero, neither increasing, which would be a positive slope, nor decreasing, which would be a negative slope. If *x* is positive, it looks like the tangent line is increasing, a positive number. Indeed, that's what we find out; a positive number raised to the fifth power is still positive.

What happens when *x* is negative? When you raise a negative number to the fifth power, is it positive or negative?

Rob: Negative.

Andy: Right. You get a negative number, and that shows up here in the fact that the derivative, that is the slope of the tangent, the tangent line has negative slope. *F* prime of *x* is less than zero on this side. The derivative is greater than zero on that side.

Lesson 6-B

Andy: Yes, Doug?

Doug: I'm a little confused about *h*. It, what, what does it have to do with anything here? It seems to disappear.

Andy: The question is, what is the role of *h* in the definition of the derivative. Because it doesn't appear in the answer, what is it doing there. Let me put the formula back up and draw you a picture that'll show you what it's doing there.

Here is the beginning of a typical graph. It consists of an *x*-axis, set horizontally and the *f* of *x*-axis, sometimes called the *y*-axis, in many cases you would have *y* equal to some function of *x* on the vertical axis here, and then the function would say at each value of *x*, what is your value of *f* of *x*? What is your height at a given value of *x*?

Let me draw you one such function, out of many many. Any way that you could draw a curve along here, as long as you never came back on yourself, as long as each value of *x* gave you only one value for the function, that would be a perfectly good function, and let's call this the particular value *x*, at which we wish to find the derivative. The role of the *h* which you've asked about, is to give us a second point. It takes two points to determine a line. There are many many lines through one point, but only one line through two distinct points. So let's move out here a distance *h*, and that will bring us to the value (*x* plus *h*) which you see up here in the numerator. Let's take the function value at (*x* plus *h*), which is the height here. The *f* of (*x* plus *h*) minus the *f* of *x*, which is this height, subtracting that height off gets us the numerator in our equation for the derivative, and dividing by *h*, which is the base of our triangle here, gives us the slope of this tangent line.

Excuse me, let me correct myself, the slope of the secant line connecting these two points. This is the slope of (*f* of [*x* plus *h*] minus *f* of *x*) divided by *h*. The notation here at the left, limit as *h* goes to zero says, we don't want that for a particular *h*. We don't want to know how far you went in a whole hour. We want to know your speed, say right now at one exact point. So what we're going to do is let that *h* get smaller. If we make it half as large, we get a different line passing through the original point here and one other, and in the limit as *h* tends to zero, we will have a line that's exactly tangent to the curve, just like this one is. This is the tangent line and the fact is, the slope of the tangent line is the same as the derivative. That's an important idea. The slope of this tangent line equals the derivative *f* prime of *x*. Any time you hear the word derivative, think in your mind, if you had a graph of that function, we're talking about how steep that is. That is, the curve is steeper here, it has a steeper tangent, and the derivative is measuring the steepness of the curve there.

So I hope I've answered your question about ...

Lesson 6-C

June: So what we have here is we have a scale, where the appearance of the duck is rated on a scale from zero actually all the way up to twenty (we only observe values between four and sixteen), and we've also got observations on the behavior of ducks, scaled in the same way; smaller values correspond to being more like a mallard, larger values correspond to being more like a pintail and we have this particular scatter plot.

What can we see? When you make a plot of two variables, what you want to do is stand back away from your plot and look at its basic shape. When I look at this plot I see a cloud of points, that is basically oval in shape with the oval pointing from lower left to upper right. That means to me that ducks that had a higher plumage rating tended also to have a higher behavioral rating. Ducks that had a lower plumage rating tended also to have a lower behavioral rating.

Let's skip for right now onto the next plot, the plot that's labeled demographics on your handout. And this particular plot depicts data, ah, from various countries. We have on the horizontal axis the percentage...

...so the first plot, the oval-shaped pointing upward look like this, oval-shaped pointing downward look like this, and round are just round...

...so let's label these: This one's got, what kind of correlation?

Wade: Positive.

June: Positive. OK. This one's got?

Tim: Negative.

June: Negative correlation. This one's got?

Tim: Little.

June: Little correlation, if any. And this one?

Kathryn: Positive.

June: ...is again positive. Great....

...one of the things that we can tell by looking at these plots is for these three plots that have noticeable correlation, the basic relationship between the two variables is linear. If I draw a line it pretty well describes the relationship with a little bit of scatter around the lines. What we'd like now to look at is something that will measure, say, the difference between this plot and this plot. Here we see for the housing data, that the points are all really tightly clustered around the line, whereas for the ducks data the points are really less tightly clustered around the line. So we'd like to come up with...

...in fact, if we look at the plots that we have, I can give you the correlation coefficients. For the ducks the correlation coefficient was computed to be plus .825; for the demographics, the correlation coefficient was minus .86, so pretty close in magnitude but of opposite sign. For the baseball data, the correlation coefficient was minus .03, very close to zero as we would have suspected; and for the housing prices, the correlation coefficient was .98, very close to one, indicating, as was pointed out, that really the points very nearly fall on a line.

Lesson 6-D

Daphne: Hold on just a sec. Wait, what were you gonna say about...

Barbara: Marketing, like, like your advertising policies would be influenced a lot by government.

Daphne: OK. Uh, huh. Can you give an example of that?

Barbara: Well, I don't imagine that if, you know, you were selling to Peoples' Republic of China that you could depend a lot on TV advertising videos or anything, I mean...

Daphne: OK.

Barbara: ...whereas in Japan, right?

Daphne: OK, so, so TV ownership...

Unit 7: Student Questions 1

Lesson 7-A

Andy: Before we move along to a more general interpretation of the derivative, are there any questions at this point? Yes, Doug.

Doug: I'm a little confused about h, it, what, what does it have to do with anything here. It seems to disappear.

Andy: The question is what is the role of h in the definition of the derivative. Because it doesn't appear in the answer, what is it doing there. Let me put the formula back up and draw you a picture that'll show you what it's doing there.

Here is the beginning of a typical graph. It consists of an x-axis...

Lesson 7-B

Andy: So I hope I've answered your question about the role of h in the definition and at the same time I hope I've given you some more graphical intuition behind what the derivative is and how to think about it. Yes, Bill.

Bill: Does it matter how big h is? It seems that if you go any amount uh, to h and then work backwards, um, it should give you the same tangent line. Is that right?

Andy: The question is, does it matter how big *h* is. Um, it would seem that whatever *h* is, as you work your way back toward zero you'll get the same answer. That is exactly right. Your intuition is correct. Um, the derivative has to be defined as a limit because for different *h*s you have different slopes here, but as *h* tends to zero, in that limit you'll just have one answer left, and that answer is the tangent line.

Lesson 7-C

Bill: Um, my question is about the falling object that we talked about. Um, I've always heard that there's a limit to how fast things can fall but this seems to indicate that there is no limit, that, um, the rate is always going to be sixteen times something, um, that it's a standard. Is that right?

Andy: The question is, my example here of the falling object which falls 16*x* squared feet after *x* seconds after being dropped and has a speed of 32 times *x* feet per second *x* seconds after being dropped. The question is, that doesn't seem reasonable because it appears to increase without limit. And let me just say, you're absolutely right, I should have said that this example applies in a vacuum only and that in real life, in the real world there is something called air resistance which acts against the pull of gravity and causes a falling object to reach what's called a terminal velocity which is its steady state at which the gravitational force pulling downward exactly balances the air resistance which is retarding it by pushing upward so this is only meant to apply for the first, say, few seconds and would be more complicated after that.

Lesson 7-D

Daphne: Now, the other thing that you can think about, though, are functional features. And, um, we just talked about some of those things, uh, the primary function, for the bicycle in, in the U.S., versus the bicycle in China is completely different. In the U.S., the primary function really for most bicycle users is for pleasure, or for sports, exercise. The primary function of a bicycle in China is, of course, transportation, so that primary function is different and of course, secondary functions might be different also. Can you think of any examples of what, you know, sort of a secondary function might be?

Barbara: In China, or in the States?

Daphne: Either.

Barbara: Uh huh, well, transportation in a way is secondary here, isn't it?

Daphne: OK, so...

Barbara: ...to recreation.

Daphne: Yeah, so that would be a secondary function here, uh huh. I think that another thing might be, um, well, in China for example, carrying things, um, you would definitely need a basket. You're either carrying other, you know, children or you're carrying, um, groceries home, things like that, so that that affects the basic design of your product, if you're going to need to, to make the bike stable with heavy things on the back, you know, obviously...

Bob: Functional features: do you mean additional features to the bike?

Daphne: A feature that affects the way it's used, yeah, the way it functions. So that if it functions to carry, um, groceries and things like that then it has to have certain attributes just because of that function. OK? The third thing to think about...

Lesson 7-E

Daphne: ...and the, oh yeah, Barbara.

Barbara: If you think about tires for example,

Daphne: Mm hmm.

Barbara: ...you know these wide tires are now popular on American bikes. Would you classify this as a functional feature or a design feature in that case?

Daphne: Um, what are those bikes used for most? I mean what's their feature?

Barbara: That's a good question. It seems to have a whole variety of needs. Some people use them as transportation and you know they call them city bikes and, uh, it seems to be a design thing too. I don't know. I'm not a bicyclist!

Daphne: Well, I think that what really happens in terms of the market place, especially in the United States is that a functional need can influence the whole perception that the market has and then it becomes a status need.

Barbara: Or vice versa.

Daphne: Right, exactly. So that, um, people

might have originally started using the um heavier duty bikes um in the United States that are popular now because they really, the others weren't really rugged enough and didn't hold up well enough. But now it's, everyone, it's, you know it's produced a whole different, it's opened up a whole new market for bicycle manufacturers.

Barbara: Same thing with the clothing, isn't it?

Daphne: Sure, yeah. Yeah.

Lesson 7-F

Barbara: Certainly your whole marketing plan.

Daphne: OK.

Jim: You couldn't export guns to Japan.

Daphne: Hold on just a sec, wait, what were you gonna say about...

Barbara: Well, marketing, like your advertising policies would be influenced a lot by the government.

Daphne: OK, uh huh. Can you give an example of that?

Barbara: Well, I don't imagine that if you know, you were selling to Peoples' Republic of China that you could depend a lot on TV advertising videos or anything, I mean...

Daphne: OK.

Barbara: ...you know, whereas in Japan! Right?

Daphne: OK, so TV ownership, um, is important. Um, also, um, we were talking about government regulations that um TV ownership isn't exactly part of government regulations, but it certainly affects your advertising capabilities, um, but the other thing that would be a government regulation is, is whether or not you can mention another product. So referring to another product. Do you remember when that wasn't allowed in the U.S.? When you couldn't do that; now all of a sudden they can refer to those others directly? OK.
  Um, Jim, you had something that you were gonna mention.

Jim: I, you can't, I was thinking, you can't export guns to Japan.

Becky: I was thinking of that too.

Jim: Guns are not legal, um, so I was just, I don't know what kind of category you'd call that but uh...

Daphne: OK, so legal...

Jim: Legality, yeah.

Daphne: ...illegal goods. Or alcohol to Saudi Arabia.

Jim: Right. Right.

Unit 8: Student Questions 2

Lesson 8-A

Andy: Class, because this graph is so important to the material we've covered, I'd like to just pause and make sure everyone understands it. Are there any questions about this graph and the tangent?

Lesley: Yeah, where'd you get your hair cut?

Andy: My hair cut? Actually, my wife cut it. But let's get back to the material. Any questions about this graph please? OK, let's move on then.

Lesson 8-B

Andy: Are there any questions at this point?

Cynthia: Um, is this gonna be on the exam?

Andy: Um, this is crucial material, in fact, for the course, so you can expect everything that we've covered so far to be on the test.

Lesson 8-C

June: Are there any more questions about these correlation examples? Yes?

Cynthia: Could you go over the homework? Especially number four?

June: OK, well let's finish up this material for right now and perhaps we can deal with this at the end of the hour or you can come by my office and we'll go over it in office hours.

Lesson 8-D

Andy: Are there any questions? Yes, Andrew.

Andrew: Yeah, what if you already have the derivative.

Andy: I'm sorry, I don't understand the question.

Andrew: Oh, I mean what if the derivative is all you've got.

Andy: Hmm. I'm still not sure what you mean. Can you think of a different way of asking that?

Andrew: Well, suppose you have a derivative, um, but you don't know the original equation.

Andy: I see, so you're asking, suppose you're given a derivative and you're asked to find the original function.

Andrew: To go backwards, yeah.

Andy: Right, to go backwards. OK, that's advanced material. We'll be covering that in about two weeks. I'll just say two brief things about it now since you bring it up. Um, first of all, it's more complex and the answer doesn't always exist the way it does for taking a derivative. And secondly, I'll give you just the simple formula for one case which is, if the derivative is a power of x, say the nth power, then the original function that has that as its derivative would be x to the (m plus 1) over (m plus 1) plus any arbitrary constant. And you can convince yourself easily that this works. When you take the derivative of this function, the derivative of a constant is zero, so that won't be in there,... the (m plus 1) will come down and cancel the denominator, subtracting one will leave you with the x to the nth power.

Andrew: Uh huh.

Andy: But we'll do more on that in a few weeks.

Andrew: OK.

Lesson 8-E

June: So, are there any questions? Yeah.

Elisabeth: Well what if it's just a line.

June: Um, if all the points fall exactly on a line the correlation coefficient will be either plus or minus one. Is that what you mean?

Elisabeth: No, what if the graph is just a line?

June: I'm not quite sure I understand what you're asking. Perhaps you could point it out to me on the handout, what you mean.

Elisabeth: Ah, well, what... no, never mind.

June: No, no, let's, I think, I'm sure you've got a good question here, let's, let's pursue it.

Elisabeth: Well, what if it were just a line like this?

June: Oh, that's a very good question. Yes, what if, your question is, what if all the points fell on a horizontal line. Then the correlation coefficient will turn out to be zero in that case.

Lesson 8-F

June: Are there any more questions? Yes.

Rob: Well, what if you have some kind of extra point.

June: If you have some kind of an extra point, um, can you elaborate?

Rob: Well, you know, an extra point, like on, on the housing graph.

June: Um hmm? Yes?

Rob: Well, like suppose there's one house that's really expensive even though it's small.

June: Oh, that's a very good question. Ah, in that case the point is called an outlier and actually that's something I'd like to defer talking about until next lecture, but we will get to it in the next, next lecture.

Rob: OK.

Unit 9: Brainstorming

Lesson 9-A

Daphne: Um, think about a product. And in any product you have the core component. Let's say we're talking about bicycles. And you're a French company with a bicycle that you're marketing. What's the name of a French bicycle?

Jim: Peugeot?

Daphne: Peugeot, yeah. OK, so you're Peugeot and you are marketing a bicycle. The most important question to ask is, what need, what need does it satisfy. So, if you are a French company bringing a bicycle into the United States, what need would that bicycle satisfy? What does the customer need a bicycle for in the United States?

Kate: Transportation?

Daphne: Transportation.

Barbara: Recreation?

Becky: Leisure?

Daphne: Leisure.

Jim: Fashion?

Daphne: Fashion?

Jim: Well...

Daphne: Maybe.

Jim: Well, you'd want to get a French bicycle because it's from France. You know, we have this thing in our head that says that...

Daphne: OK, so status. It might have a certain amount of status involved with it. OK. And how would that differ from the same French company taking the bicycle to China? What's, what need does a bicycle satisfy in China?

Becky: Everyday transportation.

Daphne: Uh huh. OK, so you see a clear difference in, in the terms of the basic function of a bicycle in those two different markets. So...

Lesson 9-B

Daphne: Now, what other things do you think that you have to consider when you take a product abroad? Think of some examples that you might know of, of companies that have gone overseas.

Kate: The government regulations...

Daphne: OK.

Kate: ...of the country you're going into.

Daphne: Uh huh. What, what types of things do those government regulations affect?

Kate: Price.

Daphne: OK. So they would affect price, mm hmm, and that's something that we're going to talk a lot about in the next couple of weeks. What else?

Kate: Where you could actually do the manufacturing.

Daphne: OK, OK.

Kate: Whether you could do it within the country, or whether you'd import it.

Daphne: Mm hmm.

Barbara: Certainly your whole marketing plan.

Daphne: OK.

Jim: You couldn't export guns to Japan.

Daphne: Hold on just a sec, wait, what were you gonna say about...

Barbara: Well, marketing, like your, your advertising policies would be influenced a lot by the government.

Daphne: OK. Uh huh. Can you give an example of that?

Barbara: Well, I don't imagine that if you know, you were selling to Peoples' Republic of China that you could depend a lot on TV advertising videos or anything, I mean...

Daphne: OK.

Barbara: ...you know, whereas in Japan! Right?

Daphne: OK, so TV ownership, um, is important. Um, also, um, we were talking about government regulations that um TV ownership isn't exactly part of government regulations, but it certainly affects your advertising capabilities, um, but the other thing that would be a government regulation is, is whether or not you can mention another product. So referring to another product....

...so what other things can you think of—other, perhaps other cultural factors that influence taking your product abroad? Can you think of anything else?

Bob: Um, competition with another product. An existing product.

Daphne: OK.

Bob: Like you said a Cuisinart is competing with a small space and chopping knife, or some other, um...

Daphne: OK, so you're thinking of competition, you're also thinking of substitute products.

Bob: Substitute products.

Daphne: Uh huh.

Kate: Also the disposable income of the market that you're selling to.

Daphne: OK.

Lesson 9-C

Daphne: Um, we're going to do, um, look at this in a lot more detail, and in your reading for tomorrow, um, there's a great diagram that I'd like for you to look at that's all about, um, the extended product model. And it really looks at a lot of different areas that you need to consider, uh, depending on your product.

Um, when you do that reading, I'd also like it if you would think about our local products here. Um, what are some things that you can think of that you might be trying to export from Washington State.

Barbara: Washington wine!

Daphne: OK, wine. OK, you can take wine. What else?

Bob: Apples.

Daphne: Apples? OK.

Kate: Wood?

Daphne: Wood?

Kate: ...wood products.

Becky: Salmon.

Daphne: Salmon. Jim?

Jim: Yeah, I'm just...

Daphne: Timber. How about timber? OK, so each one of you think about one of those, those, those areas, and as you're going through, actually, think about some of the products, the problems that you might encounter when you take that product abroad. OK. That's all for today, so see you next week.

Unit 10: Problem Solving

Lesson 10-A

Andy: That definition is very exact, very precise, and yet very cumbersome. So in fact we have a few simple rules for finding a derivative in special cases, so we don't have to go to that rather messy definition.

First of all, if you have a function that takes the particular form simply some power of x, say x to the nth power, then the derivative, after going through many steps through the definition, you would find a very simple relationship. The derivative of this function is n times x to the (n minus one).

So one application of that rule might be as follows: Suppose, for example, f of x is x to the sixth power. What would the derivative of that be, class?

Rob: $6x$ to the fifth.

Andy: $6x$ to the fifth. That's correct. How did you do that?

Rob: Well, you take the factor, the, uh, 6, x to the sixth power, you multiply the x by 6, subtract one from the exponent, whatever it is, which is, uh, 6 minus one would be 5, so you have $6x$ to the fifth.

Andy: Good. In other words, you did exactly what the formula said: Take the exponent, multiply it here, and take one less than the power. Very good. Let me give the two other rules, in review...

Lesson 10-B

Andy: Let's apply this graph to the example we did just a moment ago. When you carefully plot the function x to the sixth power, you find something that rises very steeply on both sides. Because it's an even power, you get a positive number even when x is a negative number because it's multiplying by itself. The derivative here $6x$ to the fifth: what is that derivative when x is zero? Class?

Ann: Zero?

Andy: Right. When you plug in zero for x, you get a derivative of zero. Here at x equals zero, here at the origin, we verify that the tangent line is indeed horizontal, that is to say, it has a slope of zero, neither increasing, which would be a positive slope, nor decreasing, which would be a negative slope. If x is positive, it looks like the tangent line is increasing, a positive number. Indeed, that's what we find out; a positive number raised to the fifth power is still positive.

What happens when x is negative? When you raise a negative number to the fifth power, is it positive or negative?

Rob: Negative.

Andy: Right. You get a negative number, and that shows up here in the fact that the derivative, that is the slope of the tangent, the tangent line has negative slope. F prime of x is less than zero on this side. The derivative is greater than zero on that side.

Lesson 10-C

June: The final plot for today's lecture depicts prices of houses in a particular small town, plotted against the square footage as a measure of the size of the house. What do you see in this plot?

Andrew: As square footage increases, so does the price.

June: As square footage increases, so does the price. Definitely. When we have higher values of square footage, we also have higher values of price. How would you describe the basic shape of this plot?

Andrew: A line?

June: It's pretty close to a straight line, not exactly a straight line, I'd actually say it's again oval, but a skinny oval. Much skinnier than the other ovals that I've drawn.

Lesson 10-D

June: When we look at plots and we notice that we have basically an oval-shaped scatter diagram pointing upwards, we say that the scatter plot, scatter diagram is depicting positive correlation. So here we've got positive correlation, or we can say that the two variables, plumage and behavior, are positively correlated. If the scatter diagram is pointing downward, we say we've got negative correlation and if we're in the third case and we have a round nebulous cloud of points with no clear orientation, pretty much what we can say about the correlation is that there is very little or perhaps no correlation.

So let's label these: This one's got, what kind of correlation?

Wade: Positive.

June: Positive. OK. This one's got?

Tim: Negative.

June: Negative correlation. This one's got?

Tim: Little.

June: Little correlation, if any. And this one?

Kathryn: Positive.

June: ...is again positive. Great. Very good.
So now we have some idea about the direction of correlation, positive or negative. We can also look at...

Lesson 10-E

Daphne: Can you think of any ways that you can, um, if you're, if you're trying to market something, you as a, somebody in the United States trying to market something in, uh, China. How would you find out about disposable income? Where would you go to find that information?

Kate: Um, in that case I'd assume there'd be some numbers from the government somewhere.

Daphne: Yeah.

Kate: I'd have to rely on government data. I don't think you could find it...

Daphne: Yeah, there, there's a lot of information like that available and it's, it's really fairly easy to find. Um, even in the library here we have these rooms that are just full of that kind of information, so, yeah, you could find that...

Unit 11: Discussion

Lesson 11-A

Daphne: Um, Jim, you had something that you were gonna mention.

Jim: I, you can't, I was thinking, you can't export guns to Japan.

Becky: I was thinking of that too.

Jim: Guns are not legal, um, so I was, I don't know what kind of category you'd call that but...

Daphne: OK, so legal...

Jim: Legality, yeah.

Daphne: ...illegal goods. Or alcohol to Saudi Arabia.

Jim: Right. Right.

Becky: I can't remember exactly what the products were but um, we tried to export some things to Japan, things that we use every day and they bombed in Japan. Can you remember what any of those are? Like things we use every day here in the Western World...

Jim: No, I was just wondering...

Becky: ...was a big thing in Japan so we, so some of the companies tried to export it and it just bombed flat. I can't think of it. Maybe hamburger makers or, I'm not sure what, what the products were but in a sense, you need to consider the culture and the daily activities, like is this product gonna even find its place, you know?

Jim: Yeah.

Barbara: That's true, but that advertising is also a strong factor there. I've heard somewhere, for example, if you're in Japan, they won't let you advertise your cars, American cars, in Japanese; they have to be advertised in English and so you're not, you know, the Japanese aren't going to get the information about the product that, you know, they would if it were in their own language, I mean, so what? Is that 'cause the product bombs? Or is that a result of being, um, having restricted advertising regulations?

Daphne: Right, so they, they interrelate, a lot, these things.

Unit 12: Putting Students to Work

Lesson 12-A

Andy: Now, I'd like some volunteers of people to do the homework problems at the board. Volunteers please? Um, OK, well, let's see. Rob, why don't you do number one at this part of the board. Elisabeth, please do number two here in the middle, and um, OK, Cindy, please do number three right over here.

OK, thank you, thank you, thank you. Let's look at number one here. F of x is $3x$ plus 17, f prime of x, derivative is 3. Does everyone agree with that answer? Anyone disagree? That is correct. To tidy things up here, I would be careful to write that beginning here is the derivative, so we don't get confused and think this is still equal to the original function, but you have the right answer there.

Over here for number two, if f of x is x squared plus x, the claim is the derivative f prime of x is $2x$. Please raise your hand if you agree. Um, please raise your hand if you disagree. Do we have, ah, another answer to that? What is it please, Lesley.

Lesley: $2x$ plus one.

Andy: $2x$ plus one. Let's look at that and see. The x squared would give us a $2x$ bringing the 2 down, 2 minus 1 is 1 for the first power, and this x is really x to the first power. It's not a constant so it doesn't disappear and you do need that extra term. So the correct answer to this one is indeed $2x$ plus one. Thank you, Lesley.

For number three, if f of x is x to the fifth plus $4x$ minus 2, the derivative is ($5x$ to the fourth) plus 4. Does everyone agree on that one? Any different answers? OK, that one is in fact correct. Again just to tidy up the notation here, let's be careful and write an equals sign in between so it doesn't look like those symbols are running into each other.

Lesson 12-B

June: Now I have some work that I'd like you to do here in class. I'd like you to form yourselves into pairs or if there's an odd person, you can have a triple. Here's the assignment. It's a set of data about how broad trees are at their bases and we'll look at how well it's correlated with how large the tree is in terms of volume. Each pair should take a white sheet and a yellow sheet. Use the yellow sheet to draw your graph on, and then go ahead and answer the questions that are on the handout. So form yourselves into pairs; you might as well work with the person sitting next to you.

OK, I think you've all had enough time, or most of you have had enough time to finish with the lab work. Let's discuss the, some of the answers now. I think we'll start, we'll just, ah, go around the room and the different groups can give me answers to the questions.

What's the basic shape of the plot that you've created?

Andrew: Ah, virtually a line. Almost a line.

June: Yeah, it's very nearly a line. Very good. How about the next question. Is the correlation coefficient positive, negative, or near zero?

Cynthia: Positive.

June: Great! Positive. Now, is, are the correlation coefficient nearer to minus one, zero, or plus one?

Ann: Plus one?

June: Great. Plus one. Very good.

Unit 13: One on One

Lesson 13-A

Andy: So, how can I help you, Laura?

Laura: Well, I missed your lecture on derivatives and I'm pretty much lost. I don't, I haven't the slightest clue how to do the, start the homework. So I was wondering if you could explain to me briefly, um, give me some pointers. I'm really lost. I read someone else's notes but they didn't seem to help much.

Andy: Well, I guess the question is probably, how do you apply the basic rules,

Laura: OK.

Andy: ...for taking derivatives. To do that, I imagine you have those rules in your notes, probably what we should do is work through a couple of examples.

Laura: OK. Good.

Andy: OK, um, these are problems like what are due on the homework...

Laura: Mm hmm.

Andy: ...and um, let's just start with number one here. They tell us that the function f of x is three x squared...

Laura: Mm hmm.

Andy: ...and the problem is to find the derivative...

Laura: OK.

Andy: ...f prime of x.

Laura: And the derivative is the rate of change, am I right?

Andy: That's right.

Laura: OK. OK.

Andy: And, that's what it is conceptually...

Laura: Mm hmm.

Andy: ...that doesn't help you do it in a real problem.

Laura: Oh.

Andy: To do real problems you have to apply the basic formulas.

Laura: OK.

Andy: And like learning how to ride a bicycle, it's something that you try a few times and then it's, it's a natural thing to do.

Laura: Oh.

Andy: You learn by doing, basically. So, taking this $3x$ squared, um, the first part, 3 is just a constant...

Laura: Mm hmm

Andy: ...so you might as well just write down "f prime of x equals" on the next line...

Laura: Mm hmm... prime of x...

Andy: ...and, in fact you'd put the prime on the f here.

Laura: OK.

Andy: And cross out the prime under the x. Good. And that stands for the derivative of the function f of x.

Laura: OK.

Andy: The derivative of a power of x, say x to the n...

Laura: Mm hmm

Andy: ...is equal to that power n times x raised to the n minus one, that is you bring the power out front...

Laura: Mm hmm

Andy: ...and then you subtract one and use that for the exponent.

Laura: So squared, subtract one from here?

Andy: Mm hmm

Laura: So it's three just x prime?

Andy: To the first power.

Laura: x to the first power—OK.

Andy: So you could put a one there. And don't forget bringing your power out front also.

Laura: Two, OK, so it's two times three?

Andy: That's right.

Laura: OK, so, two times three here, so six x.

Andy: Right. And do you know what *x* to the first power is?

Laura: Just the same as *x*.

Andy: Right.

Laura: Right.

Andy: So what's the final answer then?

Laura: Um, six.

Andy: What happened to your *x* to the one?

Laura: Um...

Andy: You just told me that *x* to the one is *x*.

Laura: Right, so it's six *x*.

Andy: Good. That is the final answer.

Laura: OK.

Andy: Put a box around it.

Laura: Bravo!

Andy: Let's move on to the next one! Um, let's do number three next. That looks pretty straightforward.

Laura: OK. *F* of *x* equals *x* cubed. OK, so I bring this power, this is, um, *n* minus one, so this is gonna change into two?

Andy: Mm hmm.

Laura: And there's nothing to bring, no, I bring this out here. Three and then *x* squared?

Andy: Very good. That's the answer.

Laura: OK, got it!

Andy: Now, why don't you write *f* prime of *x* equals...

Laura: *F* prime of *x* equals three *x* squared.

Andy: Good. Because that's a complete statement that the derivative of the function is your answer.

Laura: OK.

Andy: Good. Let's try a harder one... [time passes]

Andy: ...perfect!

Laura: Great. Well I think I understand it now.

Andy: OK. I think you're in good shape.

Laura: Thanks!

Lesson 13-B

Cara: So how can I help you today, Leslie?

Leslie: Well, I had a question about the lecture.

Cara: Mm hmm.

Leslie: You said we should use "da" in "Kyoto wa kidei machi da to omou," but we can't use "da" in "Kyoto wa chikai to omou."

Cara: Right, it should be "Kyoto wa chikai to omou."

Leslie: Yeah.

Cara: Yeah.

Leslie: But why?

Cara: Oh, so you're wondering why is it sometimes we use "da" and sometimes there's no "da" with the "tomo"?

Leslie: Yeah, if, if "da" translates to "is."

Cara: Yeah, good question. Um, how about if I give you some examples. Um.

Leslie: OK.

Cara: How about this sentence: um, "Kyoto wa furui to omou." Do you hear a "da" in there?

Leslie: No.

Cara: And then translate that into English.

Leslie: It means "Kyoto's an old city"?

Cara: Yeah.

Leslie: I think?

Cara: Mm hmm, or "Kyoto is old," right?

Leslie: Oh, "Kyoto is old," yeah.

Cara: Yeah. How about another one: "Kyoto wa chiisai to omou." Do you hear a "da"?

Leslie: No.

Cara: 'Kay, I'll say it again: "Kyoto wa chiisai to omou." What's that in English?

Leslie: "Kyoto is small," I think.

Cara: Yeah, small, yeah. Um, one more. First of all, do you hear a "da" or not: "Kyoto wa yasui to omou."

Leslie: "I think Kyoto is cheap."

Cara: Yeah. Did you hear a "da"?

Leslie: No.

Cara: Yeah. What do all of these words have in common: Near, old, small, cheap?

Leslie: They're, they're all adjectives.

Cara: OK, I'm gonna write that down. And none of them use the "da" with the "tomo." Yeah. How about this sentence? Um, first of all, do you hear a "da" in there? "Kyoto wa yumei na machi da to omou."

Leslie: There's a "da".

Cara: Yeah, and how would you translate that?

Leslie: Um, "I think Kyoto is a famous city"?

Cara: Mm hmm, famous city. How 'bout "Kyoto wa kirei na basho da to omou." Do you hear a "da" in there?

Leslie: No.

Cara: "Kyoto wa kirei na basho da to omou."

Leslie: "I think Kyoto is a pretty place."

Cara: Yeah, and what was the first question? "Kirei na machi." OK. Um, what's the difference between "famous city," "pretty place," and then words like near, old, small, cheap?

Leslie: Well, this one's a noun phrase and these are adjectives.

Cara: Yeah, exactly. So what do you think about the use of "da"?

Leslie: You mean, you can only use it with, with noun phrases?

Cara: Mm hmm.

Leslie: Is that right?

Cara: Yeah. I'm going to write that down, here, um, so if I asked you to translate into Japanese, "I think Kyoto is old," how might you translate it?

Leslie: "Kyoto wa furui to omou"?

Cara: Yeah. And how 'bout, um, "I think Kyoto is a famous city."

Leslie: "Kyoto wa yumei na machi to omou"?

Cara: Try again.

Leslie: "Da to omou"?

Cara: Yeah, yeah, why, why "da"?

Leslie: 'Cause it's a noun phrase.

Cara: Yeah, 'kay, um, how about us writing a rule then. What do you think the rule would be, for the "da"?

Leslie: Um, you use "da" if the complement is a noun phrase?

Cara: OK. That sounds good. You use "da" if the complement is a noun phrase. OK. Do you want to test that?

Leslie: How?

Cara: Um, let's talk about people, for example. I'll give you a sentence in English and you translate it into Japanese, OK?

Leslie: OK.

Cara: "I think he is a doctor."

Leslie: Uh, "Kare wa isha to omou."

Cara: OK, is a doctor a noun or a...

Leslie: "...isha da to omou."

Cara: Yeah, yeah, yeah! Can you do it again? "I think he is a doctor"?

Leslie: "Kare wa isha da to omou."

Cara: Yeah, because doctor is a noun and that's correct. "Kare wa isha da to omou."

Leslie: Hmm.

Cara: Yeah, um, how about, let's see, we've done other reporting words, other than "think," right? Did we use um, "kiita," I heard?

Leslie: Mm hmm.

Cara: OK. How about "I heard he is an American."

Leslie: Um, "Americajin da to kiita."

Cara: Yeah perfect, because "an American" is a noun...

Leslie: Mm hmm.

Cara: ...and you'd use the "da." How 'bout "I heard he is kind."

Leslie: Um, "Shinsetsu," that's a nonnominal.

Cara: Yeah, perfect.

Leslie: So you use "da" because it's a noun.

Cara: Yeah, so what would it be? "Kare wa..."

Leslie: Uh, "...shinsetsu da to kiita."

Cara: Mm hmm. So in English, even though it's

an adjective, the word *kind,* in Japanese it's really a nominal.

Leslie: Yeah.

Cara: So we'd use the "da." Great.

Leslie: Yeah.

Cara: How do you feel about that?

Leslie: Yeah, I think I understand. It's, it's adjectives and verbs follow one pattern...

Cara: Mm hmm.

Leslie: ...and nominals follow the other.

Cara: Yeah. Is that pretty clear now?

Leslie: Yeah. It's real clear. Thank you.

Cara: Good for you. OK. We'll see you in class!

Leslie: OK.

Lesson 13-C

Sharon: Becky, hi. I'm glad you came. What can I help you with?

Becky: Well, you know, this story that you asked us to read. I think I got all the vocabulary and I think I, I mean I even think I understand the story. But I'm not quite sure about the assignment that you told us to do.

Sharon: You have three more days and you have to get the assignment done! OK. Um, the story, you understand the plot? What was going on with that?

Becky: I think so, yeah.

Sharon: Why don't you tell me the story in brief.

Becky: Well, I know Emma is a factory worker in a textile company and a couple years ago her father, well, her father used to work there, right?

Sharon: Yeah.

Becky: And she just found out that he had died of an overdose?

Sharon: Yeah.

Becky: Um, of veranol and that Emma was very shocked by that.

Sharon: Yeah.

Becky: And as I understand it, um, she all, she always held her father in the greatest of respect but, but not everyone in the community did. He'd been accused of stealing or something?

Sharon: Right.

Becky: ...from the company, but actually, he had told her that the owner of the company had done the stealing and blamed her...

Sharon: OK, you do have the vocabulary down. I think you understand. Um, what is the essence of what was going on?

Becky: Well, that's where I'm not sure if it's, I'm not sure if I really understand what's happening because, you know, I keep thinking about, OK, what's the main point, what's the, why did we read this. It was interesting. I like, I like it a lot...

Sharon: OK.

Becky: ...but since it feels so, I mean, I'm confused by it.

Sharon: OK, OK, maybe I can ask you some questions to kind of help you get the focus...

Becky: OK.

Sharon: ...for what I want you to do. The point of the assignment...

Becky: Yeah.

Sharon: ...is not to give me a book report. Did you understand that part?

Becky: Well I started out thinking, "OK, book report, summary," and then I thought "well, but that's what we did two years ago..."

Sharon: Yeah, right.

Becky: "...in Spanish Lit and I know she doesn't want me to do that."

Sharon: OK. Right. I want you to bring in more of your thoughts and do a little bit more of analysis of the story. OK, Emma, she killed a man...

Becky: Right.

Sharon: ...but does she feel any remorse for having done so?

Becky: Well, from what I understand, the only way she felt she could get avenge, or revenge for the fact that her father had been unrightly accused...

Sharon: Yeah.

Becky: ...was to kill the owner.

Sharon: Right. So how does she feel after she kills him?

Becky: She feels like justice has finally been done...

Sharon: OK.

Becky: ...in the only way she could do it...

Sharon: OK.

Becky: ...because the system wasn't, wasn't accommodating Emma...

Sharon: Right.

Becky: ...or her husband.

Sharon: Right. So in other words she's a tool of justice then. In her eyes.

Becky: I guess so. Yeah, in her eyes.

Sharon: OK, I mean, it was a series of things that she set up in order to reach that goal...

Becky: Right.

Sharon: ...and the goal was to avenge her father's death.

Becky: And it was like the only way she could do it, right?

Sharon: Right.

Becky: In her eyes?

Sharon: Right.

Becky: Because, I mean, if she went through the legal system, she'd be forever...

Sharon: For her own conscience.

Becky: ...crying innocence on her father's part...

Sharon: Right.

Becky: ...and Lowenthal the owner would just completely have all the power.

Sharon: Right, exactly. So, ah...

Becky: OK, well that's a, that's an interesting thing, but...

Sharon: How, OK, let's talk about justice, and let's talk about crime and, and justice. OK, as reflected in the story...

Becky: Mm hmm.

Sharon: ...and as reflected maybe in your life or in society. This society that Emma operates in is no different, say, from our Western society in the U.S.

Becky: Mm hmm.

Sharon: OK. What she did, how would that be viewed by society? Not, not her friends, not her father, and not Lowenthal. How would that be viewed by society?

[Conversation continues]

Becky: Well, I think I wanna go with truth. Because, the problem I'm having with, um, what we were talking about before with justice,...

Sharon: Yeah?

Becky: Have, having never been in Emma's position, I get, I get stopped with the killing of Lowenthal. Having not gone through what she went through to get to that point, you know?

Sharon: OK, so personally that's an offense to you?

Becky: Yeah, I, well, I just keep stopping there.

Sharon: OK.

Becky: Like, I don't know what I do. I can't relate to it. But truth—I don't know there's that, that attractive flair...

Sharon: OK, what are you going to do with that then?

Becky: Well, I'm not sure yet, but I might talk about truth and how it's difficult to define if, if possible to define, 'cause Emma's truth is different from Lowenthal's, different from her father's, different from society's.

Sharon: OK.

Becky: And um...

Sharon: OK.

Becky: I might try to take it from there but I might be back tomorrow to ask you more questions if I get stuck...

Sharon: My door is open to you.

Becky: ...if that's OK.

Sharon: Yeah, and it's not, the paper's not due until, um, next Monday.

Becky: Yeah.

Sharon: So...

Becky: So I have a few days.

Sharon: You have a few days.

Becky: Could I, if I, if this is all right.

Sharon: Mm hmm.

Becky: Could I show you maybe a basic outline in a few days?

Sharon: I'd love to see it. I'd love to. I mean I'd rather look at it to see if you're following, um, the proposal.

Becky: OK.

Sharon: OK, what I want basically...

Becky: Yeah.

Sharon: ...the proposal of what your idea, if you're following along the lines of truth. Are you gonna write this in English or Spanish?

Becky: Oh, I think I should do it in Spanish, right?

Sharon: Um, you, it's just your choice. I mean if you are really pulling things from the story, it might be easier to use Spanish because you have vocabulary and you'll be thinking already and you have that flow of thought there; if you're using English, if it's more comfortable for you, use it. Either way.

Becky: OK, well, I think at this point I'm going to try to challenge myself with Spanish.

Sharon: Fine.

Becky: And if that...

Sharon: Then by all means come in and see me before!

Becky: OK.

Sharon: Because that way, I can take care of any, um, grammatical problems or whatever. I'm not after your grammar. I really wanna know your thought process.

Becky: 'Kay, so the next time I come in, um, shall we speak in Spanish?

Sharon: Let's do it!

Becky: OK.

Sharon: OK.

Becky: Thanks a lot, Sharon.

Sharon: OK, you're welcome.

Lesson 13-D

Andy: Hello, nice to see you.

Cherie: Hi.

Andy: How can I help you?

Cherie: Well, you gave our tests back today and I didn't get a very good score and I wanted to talk it over with you. Um, you know I always do my homework and I get a good grade and I always come to class but I only got a, I only got a 70, um, and it's 'cause I couldn't finish the test. It was, it was kinda long for me and all these, all these I finished and I got them perfect, but then over here, you see, I didn't get to finish this question or these questions and I was wondering if you could, if you could just correct the ones that I finished instead of counting me off for the ones I didn't finish.

Andy: Well, let me start by, by looking over your exam and making sure the grading is correct on the, on the first few questions. It looks like these are proper. It looks like you just ran out of time as you said. Um, based on that, I'm afraid I won't be able to change your grade. It'll have to stay a 70, and what we should do instead is discuss how you can prepare yourself better for taking the final exam.

Cherie: Can I ask you one more thing? Before you do that, um, compared to other students in the class, am I the only one that didn't finish or did lots of students not finish, or...

Andy: Well, based on confidentiality of the grades of other students, I'm really not allowed to say.

Cherie: Oh. OK.

Andy: Um...

Cherie: Well, then what can I do to finish the test faster next time, 'cause I don't, I don't usually get 70s. And it, I'd like to do better next time.

Andy: Well, based on your homeworks, and what I've seen in your work outside of this exam and also based on your answers to the first few questions, it's clear you do know the material. Um, it's just a question of test-taking strategy. I think you'll have to be more careful about budgeting your time and to, to learn certain things about how to take a test efficiently in the amount of time needed. Now in some classes that doesn't matter, but in, in classes like this, the kind of mastery of the subject that we're seeking demands that, that you be able to answer things quickly.

Cherie: Um.

Andy: So let me recommend that for the next exam you read through the entire exam first and then quickly answer all those that you know right away. And only after you've done that should you go back and answer the harder and longer ones, and that'll help you get the highest score, before the time runs out.

Just one more thing, um, the other thing is there are certain basic skills that you may want to practice a little more, like being faster with the calculator.

Cherie: Oh.

Andy: And it may also help you to prepare a review sheet, maybe one or two pages that summarizes everything...

Cherie: Uh huh.

Andy: ...just to make sure that you can get quickly to that most important material.

Cherie: Well, I, I make the review sheets the weekend before the exam usually, so I do that...

Andy: Oh, good.

Cherie: ...already, but, um, I was wondering, how long do you think most students spend on the homework assignments every night?

Andy: I don't really know.

Cherie: 'Cause it, it would help me to know that because I spend about two hours and if everybody else can do that in forty-five minutes maybe I'm in the wrong class.

Andy: Well, based on...

Cherie: Maybe I should drop.

Andy: Based on your grades and the homework and on these first few questions, I would say you're doing very well. I think there's just some attention to organization and actually, some of your answers are too detailed...

Cherie: Oh.

Andy: ...and you could save time by writing a shorter answer...

Cherie: Mm hmm.

Andy: ...that would still get you full credit and that would then allow you to, to have some time to answer the later questions. In fact, um, I think you're one of the better students in the course and I would encourage you to stay in.

Cherie: So I guess I should pay more attention to the, um, points, for example if you say this one's fifteen and this one's only five—I should spend more time on the...

Andy: Oh, yes.

Cherie: ...on the fifteen point one instead of the five one.

Andy: Absolutely.

Cherie: OK, OK, well, if you think I can do better next time, I'll give it a try.

Andy: OK.

Cherie: And I'll try to pay more attention to the points and I'll try to, um, get faster with the calculator. Are there any drills or anything I can do?

Andy: Um, there is a study guide that's still available at the bookstore, if you need...

Cherie: At the bookstore? Right, OK.

Andy: ...if you need some extra questions. And part of my grading policy is, if there's one grade out of the whole course that's out of line, I try and adjust for that so that you would not be penalized unfairly...

Cherie: Oh.

Andy: ...if you do very well on the final.

Cherie: Yeah, OK, that's good. That's good to hear. That makes me feel better. OK. That's great. Thank you.

Andy: You're welcome. Good luck.

Cherie: Thanks.

Lesson 13-E

Daphne: So Tim, what can I do for you?

Tim: Well, I'm in, as you know, I'm in your international marketing seminar...

Daphne: Mm hmm.

Tim: ...and, ah, I've had to miss a few classes.

Daphne: A few?

Tim: A few, well more than a few actually, as

you know it's been a few weeks. But, ah, it's been a real tough situation um, for me, both personally and academically. It, it has to do with a sick father. My dad's been very, very ill, and it's just not been possible for me to make my classes this quarter.

Daphne: Yeah.

Tim: And I was wondering about, ah, working out an incomplete, some kind of, ah...

Daphne: An incomplete. Hmm. Well, I'm sorry about your father. I'm sorry to hear that, um, the thing is, you know, there're basically only four requirements in the course. Ah, there's a midterm and of course you could take a, you know, a make up test for that.

Tim: Oh, so I could make that up?

Daphne: Yeah, but that's the thing, the thing is that the other three projects are all team projects and of course you, I know you did the first one.

Tim: Right.

Daphne: And you did real well on that.

Tim: We did, yeah, quite well on that.

Daphne: Yeah. Yeah, but um, you know there's still, there's still, um, that only, so far, that only accounted for twenty percent of the grade. So, um, and the midterm, again that's not really very much. That's only another 25 percent of the grade. So the project that you've already missed and the one the teams are already, you know, working on and stuff, amounts to most of the course.

Tim: Yeah, well...

Daphne: And they're team projects!

Tim: Yeah, I realize that that's a problem in terms of making it up but that's why I'm here, to see if we can work something out because, um, since it's not a required course, but it is one that I need...

Daphne: Mm hmm.

Tim: ...um, to finish, I'd really like to get a grade out of the class.

Daphne: Mm hmm.

Tim: Um, and I don't know, I was thinking, these things, I mean, people do get sick and these things happen...

Daphne: Mm hmm.

Tim: ...and I was wondering if there's anything we could do, a special project perhaps, um, library research, anything at all.

Daphne: Well, you know, that wouldn't be such a problem in a different course, but because this is a seminar and especially because it's a graduate seminar, the, the work with your team is, is so important that it just really, I really couldn't accept an incomplete. It, it seems to me that you really only have, um, one option which would be to drop the course, or to withdraw from it.

Tim: Um, that seems like, I mean, having completed virtually fifty percent of the course work, that seems a little bit strong. I don't know, I was thinking, for example, if I could find other students in the program who might be willing to do the, the projects out of class with me, um, would you look at something like that?

Daphne: The students if the class are already almost finished with their final project, you know, and they've already finished one, I mean, I don't, they're not gonna want to put in extra time at this point, I'm sure.

Tim: Right, well, for example, maybe other students who are not specifically in this seminar but in the marketing program here at school, um, maybe I could find some people that, that would help me turn in something.

Daphne: Mmm. Gee Tim, I really don't think so. I, it's just, it's really too late in the quarter to try to do something like that.

Tim: Yeah, no kind of extra work or anything which could make it up, because, see, my situation, I mean, I understand your point of view, but the thing is, I mean, you never had somebody get sick before? Or a student or somebody with family problems have to leave...

Daphne: Not in this course. If, you know, if the course were a research course or, or something where you were working independently, then I could really see, see doing it better, but it's a course that really depends so totally on, on your class input and, and your work with your team members, and, um, something, you know, following a, you know, the, the major project, you know, was to follow a, a product and work with another company in the business community and it's just really too late to do any of that.

Tim: Well, yeah, I mean, I do see your side of it, um, and I'm not trying to threaten anyone or anything, but I think I'd like to talk to the chair maybe about this and see if there's something we can do.

Daphne: You can do that. That's fine.

Tim: It's not trying to be combative but I'd really like...

Daphne: No, no that's all right. I understand.

Tim: I think that I deserve a chance to get some credit for what I've done so far, and I had absolutely no control over this situation so...

Daphne: Yeah.

Tim: Um, I'd like to take this a little bit further.

Daphne: Well, that, that's fine. You're free to do that. Um, and you can write a letter to the chair and I'm sure that the chair will consider it and um...

Tim: Yeah. OK.

Daphne: But, you know, you understand my viewpoint, so...

Tim: I do, I'd rather work it out at this level between the two of us, but um, if that's not possible, um...

Daphne: Yeah.

Tim: ...then I guess that's the only option left...

Daphne: Well...

Tim: ...if, you know, I wanna keep going.

Daphne: OK.

Tim: Yeah, all right. Well, anyway, I appreciate your time.

Daphne: Sure. Yeah. Bye bye.

Tim: Bye.

Index

Active listening, 130, 132-33
American culture, discussions on, 185-88
Answering questions, strategies for, 75

Back vowels, 164
Bar graphs, 54-55, 66
Body language, 131-33
   observation assignment, 145
Brainstorming, 91-98, 199-201
   miniclass assignment, 96
   strategies for, 91

Central vowels, 164-65
Charts, pie, 57-58, 65
Classroom interaction, 73-125
Comparison, 5, 19-21
Compounds, 37-38
Comprehension
   problems, 82, 84
   strategies for, 81, 130-33
Consonants, 151-62
   /f/, 158
   /l/, 155-56
   /qu/, 158
   /r/, 154
   /th/, 151-54
   /v/, 159
   /w/, 157
Contrast, 5, 19-21

Definitions, 33-41, 192-93
   miniclass assignment, 39
Department policies, 186
Diagrams, 53-72, 194-96
   tree, 58-59
Difficult student questions, 83-90
Diphthongs, 149, 166

Directions, 122
Discussion, 107-18, 202-3
   checklist, 115-16
   leader, 107
   participation, 108-11
   miniclass assignment, 114
   observation assignment, 118
   roles in, 108-13
Discussions on American culture, 185-88

Encouraging students, 76, 101, 140
Examples, 43-51, 193-94
   miniclass assignment, 48
Exams, 188
Explaining
   graphs and diagrams, 61-66
   in office hours, 137

Formulas, 67
Front vowels, 164-65

Graphs
   bar, 54-55, 66
   line, 53-54, 63
Graphs and diagrams, 53-72, 194-96
   explaining, 61-66
   miniclass assignment, 68

Hands-on activities, 119-25, 203-4
   miniclass assignment, 123

Inappropriate student questions, 84
Individual communication, strategies for, 129-45

Information
   new, 5
   opinions versus, 113
Interaction
   classroom, 73-125
   teacher-initiated, 99-106
Intonation, question, 101-4
Introductions, 3-10, 189
   miniclass assignment, 8
ITA training, suggestions for, xii

Jargon, 33

Lax vowels, 166-67
Lecture organization, 71
Lectures, 1-72
Lesson planning (observation assignment), 71
Line graphs, 53-54, 63
Listening, active, 130, 132-33
Loudness in stressed words, 5

Main idea, stressing, 5
Maps, 64
Mathematical formulas, 67
Miniclass assignments
   brainstorming, 96
   definitions, 39
   discussion, 114
   examples, 48
   graphs and diagrams, 68
   introductions, 8
   problem solving, 104
   putting students to work, 123
   restating and summarizing, 30
   student questions, 88
   transitions, 22
Miscommunication (roleplay), 88

New information, stressing, 5

Observation assignments
  body language, 145
  discussion, 118
  lesson planning, 71
Office hours, 129–45, 204–12
  explaining in, 137
  strategies for, 129–45
Opinions versus information, 113

Pauses, 14–17, 34–35
Phonetic symbols, 149
Pie charts, 57–58, 65
Pitch, 5
Prefixes, 20
Preview, 14
Problem solving, 99–106, 201–2
  miniclass assignment, 104
Problems, comprehension, 82, 84
Pronunciation, 148–88
  dialogues
    /e/, /ɛ/, /æ/, 173
    /i/, /ɪ/, /ər/, /ear/, 170
    /o/, /a/, /ɔ/, 181
    /r/ and /l/, 156
    /th/, 152
    /u/, /ʊ/, /ʌ/, 177
    /w/, /qu/, /f/, and /v/, 160
  symbols, 149
  strategies for, 149–50
Putting students to work (miniclass assignment), 123

Question intonation, 101–4
Questions
  difficult, 83–90
  inappropriate, 85
  repeating, 75, 81
  strategies for answering, 75
  student, 14, 75–90, 196–99
  teacher-initiated, 99–106

Reduced vowels, 37
Respect, 187
Restating and summarizing, 25–32, 191–92
  miniclass assignment, 30
Review, 13–14, 25
Roleplays
  explaining in office hours, 137
  miscommunication, 88
  personal problems in office hours, 142–43
Roles in discussion, 108–13

Saying "no" politely, 141
Self-study, suggestions for, xiii
Sentence stress, 5–6, 34, 78–79, 101–4
Sound symbols, 149
Speech analysis, 7, 21, 29, 39, 47, 68, 114, 122, 142
Strategies
  answering questions, 75
  brainstorming, 91
  comprehension, 81, 130–33
  individual communication, 129–45
  office hours, 129–45
  pronunciation, 149–50
Stress
  sentence, 5–6, 34, 78–79, 101–4
  word, 36–38
Student questions, 14, 75–90, 196–99
  difficult, 83–90
  inappropriate, 84
  miniclass assignment, 88
Students, undergraduate, 185
Summarizing, 25–32, 191–92

Tables, 55–57, 62
Teacher-initiated interaction, 99–106
Teaching styles, 185
Tense vowels, 166–67

Terminology, 33–41
  multiword, 37
Tests, 188
Time management, 186
Transcripts, 189–212
Transition words, 14, 17–19
Transitions, 13–24, 189–91
  miniclass assignment, 22
Tree diagrams, 58–59

Undergraduate students, 185
Universities around the world, 187

Verb tense, in summaries, 26
Video, xi
Video transcripts, 189–212
Visual aids, 59
Vocabulary planners, 8–9, 22, 30–31, 40, 48–49, 69, 89, 96–97, 105, 115, 123–24
Vowel length, 5
Vowels
  /æ/, 172
  /a/, 180
  /ɔ/, 179
  back, 164
  central, 164–65
  /ɛ/, 171
  /e/, 171
  front, 164–65
  /i/, 167
  /ɪ/, 168
  lax, 166–67
  location of, 163–66
  /o/, 178
  /ər/, 169
  reduced, 37
  tense, 166–67
  /u/, 175
  /ʊ/, 175
  /ʌ/, 176

Word stress, 36–38